KEYS TO PLANNING FOR LONG-TERM CUSTODIAL CARE

David Ness
Vice President Financial Planning
Raymond James & Associates, Inc.

BARRON'S

All inquiries should be addressed to:
Barron's Educational Series, Inc.
250 Wireless Boulevard
Hauppauge, New York 11788

Library of Congress Catalog Card No. 90-27746

International Standard Book No. 0-8120-4593-9

Library of Congress Cataloging in Publication Data

Ness, David.
    Keys to long term custodial care / by David Ness.
        p.   cm.—(Barron's retirement keys)
    Includes index.
    ISBN 0-8120-4593-9
    1. Aged—Long term care—United States.   2. Retirement—
United States—Planning.   I. Title.   II. Series.
RA564.8.N45   1991
362.1′9897′00973—dc20   90-27746
                                                                    CIP

PRINTED IN THE UNITED STATES OF AMERICA
1234   5500   987654321

ACKNOWLEDGMENTS

This book is the product of the diligent efforts of many people. I am particularly grateful for the help of Lynn Sackman and the rest of the fine editorial staff at Barron's Educational Series. Also deserving of special thanks for their many hours of extra effort are Peggy Tucker of the Marketing Services Department at Raymond James and my secretary, Sally Bond. Finally, this book would not have been possible without the love, support, and considerable efforts of my wife, Terry. Thanks to you all.

CONTENTS

1

INTRODUCTION

John dropped by to see his mother Saturday afternoon. John has visited his 81-year-old mother, Mary, every week since his father died last year. John worries about his mother, but she insists she is just fine living by herself. That Saturday, John knew something was wrong when he reached the front door. His mother's mail was sticking out from the mail slot in the door. Mary always greeted the postman, an old friend, at the door and spent a few minutes chatting. When he opened the door John was greeted by the smell of smoke from Mary's breakfast that had been left burning on the stove for several hours. As John rushed into the house, he heard his mother call for help. He found Mary lying at the bottom of the basement stairs. Mary had lost her footing when she headed for the basement to change a load of laundry while cooking her breakfast. The fall broke her hip.

The moment John discovered his mother was the first time either of them considered the possibility that Mary might require some type of long-term care. The nature of the care Mary—and countless other senior citizens—may require varies according to their circumstances. Perhaps all Mary requires is some help recuperating from her broken hip. However, she may need more help with every day chores. It is also possible that Mary, either now or in the future, may require nursing home care or care in another more institutional setting. It took a crisis to open Mary and John's eyes to the problem of long-term care. You may be facing a similar crisis or you may be wisely considering alternatives well in advance of requiring care. In either case, this book is designed to provide you with guidance.

At the outset, it is important to define long-term care. There are several different levels of long-term care, some of which will be discussed later. The major focus of this book, however, is on custodial care, where the problem is most acute. As we age, we become more susceptible to the ravages of gradually debilitating conditions such as Alzheimer's disease and arthritis. In addition, sudden illnesses, such as strokes and heart attacks, can severely limit the ability to care for ourselves. The longer we live the more likely the eventuality that we may some day need help with the simplest things—walking, getting in and out of a chair, eating, and bathing. We may not need a doctor or even a registered nurse to provide care; rather we need someone with a good heart and a strong back to help us do the things we can no longer do for ourselves. This is the essence of long-term custodial care. Throughout this book the terms *long-term care, long-term custodial care,* and *custodial care* are used interchangeably.

Long-term custodial care has become a problem for two principal reasons. First, advances in health care and societal factors have increased our life expectancies. The longer we live the more likely it becomes that at least some of us will require long-term custodial care. Second, the traditional extended family structure has, to a large extent, broken down. Years ago, when Grandma needed help caring for herself, she probably lived in the same town or even in the same household as one of her children. The daughter or daughter-in-law, who did not work outside the home, provided care for Grandma as part of her daily routine. Today, Grandma's children and grandchildren are scattered across the country. If Grandma is able to move in with one of her children, the daughter or daughter-in-law probably works outside the home. The children are struggling to juggle two careers and care for a growing family of their own.

Consider the case of Bill and Debbie. Born in 1950, they have two children, Jennifer who was born in 1980 and Jason who was born in 1984. Bill's parents, Harold and Audrey, were born in 1925. Debbie's mother, Rosemary, was born in 1923; her father died last year of a heart attack. Bill and Debbie have ambitious plans to retire before they are 60 and to send their children to college. But, like so many people of their generation, they spend most of their current income. They both have careers, and most of the little saving they do goes into their companies' retirement plans. Bill's parents are in reasonably good health, although Harold, at 65, has already lived longer than both his parents and one of his brothers. Rosemary's family has a history of cancer. So far, none of them are thinking about the possibility of long-term care.

But imagine what might happen in just ten years. By then, Bill and Debbie will be 50 and ten years away from retirement. Jennifer will be 20 and in college. Jason, at 16, will be making college plans. Bill and Debbie will have at least one child in college for the next six years. Harold and Audrey will both be 75 and Rosemary will be 78, ages at which the risk for needing long-term custodial care increases. This risk will increase each year.

Bill, Debbie, and their parents have an opportunity today. They can confront the risk of long-term care and take the steps they need to cope with the problem. Some of you may not be so lucky. You may be faced with an immediate long-term care problem. You need to know what you can do *now* to protect yourself or a loved one. This book is designed to help you cope with the problem of long-term care now or in the future.

The book is organized into five basic parts. Keys 2 through 6 deal with a general outline of the planning process and the problem of long-term care. Keys 7 through 14 focus on the alternatives for seeking long-term care treatment. Keys 15 through 25 deal with payment alternatives, including long-term care insurance. Keys 26 through 34 will review some of the planning devices available to help make the transition to having someone other than yourself handle your financial and health decisions. Finally, Keys 35 through 44 give an overview of some of the important tax implications and opportunities associated with long-term custodial care.

Planning for long-term care, like any other financial planning endeavor, is best done with a team of competent and experienced advisors. This book provides a general guidance, not specific legal or tax advice. The laws in these areas can be very complex and vary from state to state. Friends, neighbors, coworkers, or relatives—unless they are experienced lawyers, accountants or financial planners—should not be relied on for advice in this area. Take the ideas from this book to an experienced advisor to find out if the ideas will work for you.

2

DEMOGRAPHIC TRENDS

According to the dictionary, a demographic trend pertains to changes in the size and composition of a population. Demographic changes can have a powerful and pervasive effect on a society. Since World War II, we have been living through one of the largest demographic changes in history, the so-called "Post-War Baby Boom." A review of this one generation's impact provides a powerful lesson for the future.

We don't need reams of statistics to recite the changes brought on by the Baby Boom generation. We remember the obstetric facilities that were added to bring them into the world and the new schools that were built to educate them. We became a youth culture, in part, because there were suddenly so many young people. Baby boomers represent the single largest portion of the population. They clog the ranks of corporate America today the same way they used to clog the halls of their schools. The eldest of the Baby Boomers are now fast approaching middle age.

It is also clear that Baby Boomers were not as prolific as their parents. There are, of course, a variety of possible explanations for this phenomenon: concerns for the environment and overpopulation, later marriages, women assuming a greater and more permanent place in the work force, and others. In many communities today, children will be unable to attend the same schools their parents attended because that school has been closed due to declining enrollment. It seems clear that the Baby Boom was followed by the "Baby Bust."

In addition to a Baby Bust, another powerful trend

is developing. The parents and grandparents of the Baby Boomers are living longer than ever before. Today's normal retirement age of 65 is older than the normal life expectancy one could have hoped for just a few decades ago. Retirement is also coming sooner. Although 65 may be considered the retirement age for some Social Security and pension purposes, many people are retiring much earlier. The corporate restructuring begun in the 1980s has accelerated this trend.

Retirement may now last for 30 years or more. Many will spend almost as much time in retirement as they did working. Retirement is also no longer always the quiet, unhurried lifestyle associated with the stereotype. As people retire sooner and remain healthy longer, many will spend a good many retirement years in pursuit of a second (or perhaps third or fourth) career, traveling, pursuing additional education, participating in recreational activities, or otherwise very actively involved in the community.

The two greatest financial risks we face during our working years are dying before accumulating enough assets to provide for our families and losing the ability to earn a paycheck because of a disability. After retirement, perhaps the greatest risk is not having enough resources to meet expenses. Many, if not most, retired people would also like to leave some type of financial legacy. Therefore, at least some assets need to be preserved for the next generation. Inflation, taxes, and poor investment decisions all can contribute to the possibility that some will outlive their money. The need for long-term care is another significant risk that affects an increasing number of people.

There are over 250 million people in the United States. About one in nine people is 65 or older; about two million to three million are 85 or older. Some experts suggest that more than six million elderly people who live at home (or with a relative) need some help with basic activities such as walking, dressing, and bathing. An additional three million or so live in nursing homes. Between 25 and 40 percent of the elderly in nursing homes are there solely for custodial services.

Studies suggest that those turning 65 today have about a 43 percent chance of requiring nursing home care before their death. The risk of requiring nursing home care increases with age. According to some figures, only about five percent of those over 65 are in nursing homes. For those 85 and older, the number increases to about 33 percent. Over 20 percent of those 85 years or older who are still at home require some regular assistance in the form of meal delivery, housekeepers, nurses, or other services.

Future prospects indicate that the problem of long-term care is likely to get worse. Some estimates indicate that by the year 2020, the number of senior citizens will double and that by 2030 (when the oldest Baby Boomers are about 85), senior citizens will represent about one in every five Americans. The "old old," or those over 85, are the fastest growing segment of the population. According to some, their numbers will just about double by the turn of the century. By 2050, the number of people 85 and over may be greater than 16 million. This powerful "graying effect" means that planning for long-term care will become a major concern to an increasing number of people.

3

THE COST OF
LONG-TERM CARE

Long-term custodial care, already expensive, is getting more expensive every day. The cost can be expressed both monetarily and emotionally. One cost can drive up the other. An elderly person can easily be hurt watching the accumulated wealth of a lifetime go to pay nursing home bills. The younger person may be forced to seek potentially expensive care to reduce the emotional burden brought on by serving simultaneously the needs of growing children and an aging parent. The burden of these costs is not easily borne, but it must be understood to plan effectively.

Health care in the United States is an enormous business; some estimate the total cost at over $600 billion per year. We pay this cost in a variety of ways. Some of it is paid directly from our checkbooks to doctors, hospitals, and other providers. Some is collected through Medicare and other taxes and dispensed to health care providers under various programs. The cost of health care is also spread throughout the economy in more subtle ways. For instance, it has been estimated that group health costs can add $700 to the price of some American-made cars. Americans pay proportionately much more for health care than the citizens of many other industrialized countries. For example, some estimates are that we spend, on a relative basis, perhaps as much as 50 percent more for health care than the Japanese or Canadians.

As we get older we are not only ill more often but those illnesses tend to be more serious, of longer duration, and more expensive. Senior citizens have been estimated to pay more than three times as much for health care each year as do younger people. Some have suggested that as many as one in five senior citizens is hospitalized annually. Long-term care can be a significant, even the most significant, contributor to the health care expenditures of senior citizens.

Nursing home costs vary widely. Broad, national averages put the current annual cost at between $22,000 and about $30,000 per year. That translates to a daily cost of about $60 to $80. Of course, the level of care (See Key 8) will have an impact on your cost. The more care that is required and the more skilled the care provider, the higher the cost. Prices also vary regionally, with areas having high real estate and labor costs obviously being generally the most expensive. Prices can also vary within a region, with rural locations tending to be less expensive than urban ones. In some cases, the source of payment can be a factor. Prices are sometimes lower for Medicaid (See Key 18) patients. The cost of nursing homes is rising faster than the general rate of inflation.

The total financial impact of a nursing home stay depends not only on the daily cost, but also on the length of stay. How long you will spend in a nursing home depends on your medical condition and other circumstances. Broad averages can be deceiving in some cases. For example, studies have put the average stay in a nursing home at about 15 months. Those studies, however, blended the experiences of people who were in a nursing home for a short period of rehabilitation with those who were permanent residents. Perhaps a more reliable statistic is the estimate that 25 percent of those turning 65 today will spend at least one year in a nursing home and nine percent will spend at least five years.

How will the cost of a nursing home stay affect your financial situation? Government studies suggest that about 50 percent of all couples could be impoverished within one year if one spouse is in a nursing home. About two out of every three single people are wiped out financially within one year after going into a nursing home. Avoiding a financial calamity is the principal reason you should plan for the possibility of long-term care.

Home health care, while generally less expensive, can also be quite costly. Part of the fee paid to a nursing home goes to cover your room and board. If you receive home health care, your basic housing costs (taxes, maintenance, utilities) may not increase. If you have trouble cooking, many communities have "Meals on Wheels" programs that can deliver at least some hot food at low or no cost. Some services, however, must be purchased. Many of these services, such as assistance in bathing or dressing, can be provided by less skilled individuals. The cost of these services varies widely, but an average range of about $7 to $10 per hour is a good guide. Skilled nursing services (i.e., those performed by a registered nurse or similar professional) can cost $20 an hour or more. The cost of home health care also varies by region, with urban areas generally much more expensive than rural areas.

The emotional cost of long-term care cannot be understated. Dealing with the long-term care needs of an elderly person is difficult for all concerned. The person receiving the care may be dependent on others for the first time since childhood. Once simple acts are now difficult or impossible. Robust, active individuals are, perhaps suddenly, restricted in their movement. The ability to engage in a favorite pastime—painting, golf, or needlepoint—may have been lost. Boredom may increase. Those who require long-term care must make adjustments, a process that may be more difficult with increased age.

All is not lost of course. One's faith and the love of family and friends among other things can ease the burden for the elderly person. But often the family also shares in the emotional cost of long-term care. Whether they provide care directly or only visit a nursing home on occasion, it is painful to have a loved one who requires long-term care. Clearly, those who provide care for aged and frail relatives bear a greater cost. Most of the home care provided to elderly people is supplied by concerned friends and family members, most of whom are women. According to some estimates, about 40 percent of those providing care are simultaneously raising a family. Surveys have concluded that over 10 percent may be forced to quit work to provide care, and over half must reduce their work hours. Nevertheless, the stereotype that too many children abandon elderly parents and other relatives in nursing homes persists. Actually, it may well be that care is provided in the home, in some cases perhaps longer than it should be, not only to save the cost of nursing home care, but also because the family feels a great sense of love and commitment to the elderly person.

Some have suggested that the older we are, the more like ourselves we become. The assertive adult may become combative. The steadfast turns stubborn. The skeptical person becomes distrustful. Mother-daughter and father-son relationships can also be difficult, even under the best of circumstances. What happens when the mother, who always "knew best," requires the daily care of her daughter? Or, consider the difficulties when the son must help his father, a man who was always "rock-steady," walk down a flight of stairs. Long-term care highlights our frailties and our mortality. As opposed to children, who grow more independent from

11

lots of love, care, and supervision, elderly people may become more dependent.

Many communities have support groups and counseling services. Some of these services may be part of the overall services provided at the health care facility. In other cases, respite care or adult day care (See Key 13) may provide some of the answers. The emotional costs of long-term care are every bit as real as the financial costs and may prove to be as difficult to pay.

4

THE FINANCIAL
PLANNING PROCESS

The famous philosopher and former catcher for the New York Yankees, Yogi Berra, once said, "If you don't know where you're going, you'll probably wind up someplace else." Financial planning is the process of figuring out where you are headed financially so that you end up where you want to be. Applying the financial planning process to the problem of long-term care can be a significant step forward in coping with the problem.

You must not only understand what financial planning is, you must understand what it is not. Financial planning is not just having someone prepare a thick book of words, numbers, and graphs. Nor is financial planning merely a justification for buying an insurance policy, limited partnership, mutual fund, or other financial product or service.

Financial planning is, first and foremost, a disciplined process for finding solutions to financial problems. It's a *process*, not an event. If you apply the process to develop an initial strategy, your work is not over; it has just begun. Financial planning is also interdisciplinary in nature. Solving personal financial problems such as long-term care requires knowledge about legal principles, tax rules, insurance policies, and financial forecasting. Significant elements of basic psychology are also involved. It may be essential for you to consult with professionals to solve long-term care problems. Key 6 discusses assembling a planning team.

The financial planning process covers two broad areas: planning for future goals and managing the risks

13

that may prevent you from attaining those goals. For example, consider the case of Mike and his wife, Carolyn. Mike and Carolyn are a young couple with three children. They may apply the financial planning process to help them attain their two principal long-term financial goals, sending their children to college and retiring at age 60. The financial planning process can also help them cope with the risks that may hinder their progress. Two of the main risks are the chance that one of them may experience a serious disability making work impossible for a significant period and that one of them may die before enough assets have been accumulated to meet their goals.

Consider, on the other hand, Tom and JoAnne's situation. They are both 65 years old and recently retired. They have worked hard, lived modestly, and accumulated a $500,000 retirement nest egg. Their goal for retirement is to travel to historical sites. The greatest risk they face is the possibility that a serious health condition, particularly one involving long-term care, will wipe out their retirement savings. A rigorous application of the financial planning process can help Tom and JoAnne meet their goal while coping with the risks.

The financial planning process involves six basic steps:
- Gather all relevant information
- Set objectives
- Evaluate the potential problems and alternative methods for achieving your objectives
- Write down your objectives and strategies
- Implement your plan
- Review the plan periodically

The first step is to gather all relevant information. Good decisions cannot be made without good information. Gather information about your assets: What are they? Where are they? How much are they worth?

How is the title held? Are they liquid (i.e., easily converted to cash)? How much income do they pay? Review your existing insurance policies: What type of coverage do you have? What are the benefits? Under what conditions will benefits be paid? Consider your liabilities: How much is owed and what are the repayment terms? When focusing on long-term care, what are your local options for seeking help and what, if any, costs are involved? Assess your family situation: Will the children be able to help? Are you willing to move to their home? What help could the children provide if called on? The more you know about your own situation, the greater the likelihood that your decisions will be wise.

The next step is to set objectives. This is an absolutely critical and often overlooked process. If you do nothing to plan for long-term care, you are implicitly expressing a willingness to risk everything on the hope that you won't have a problem. Most people would not knowingly take that risk, but many, through their inaction, already are. An example of an objective with respect to long-term care might be to accept the possibility that you would be willing to absorb the cost of up to a six-month stay at a local nursing home. You might also include in your goal that you desire to avoid the need for a court-supervised handling of your affairs and that you want to have as much say as possible about your medical care, even if you are no longer able to make medical decisions.

The next step is to evaluate the potential problems and possible alternative methods for achieving your objective. Numerous potential problems may exist. Your children may, for various reasons, be unable to provide you with much, if any, help. State laws may not allow the use of some of the planning tools that otherwise could be used to cope with long-term care needs. Your assets may not be sufficiently liquid to permit you to absorb as much of the financial burden of long-term care as you would like. These and other potential pitfalls will shape your alternatives. The various alternative strategies are discussed in Key 5 Risk Management.

Once you have selected the most appropriate strategies, write them down. This is a vital step. An unwritten goal or objective is merely a wish. In the real world, wishes don't come true. Unless you put your strategy in writing, you will forget an essential detail or overlook an important step. If you have consulted a professional financial planner, a written plan document should be a standard part of the service.

The fifth step is to implement the plan, which in itself may involve various steps. Some may involve consulting with an attorney to have documents drafted or to seek other advice. Others may involve lifestyle changes that will reduce your chances of heart disease or other illness, thus eliminating at least one possible cause of long-term care. Still other steps may involve retitling assets to take advantage of government programs. You may wish to purchase insurance policies that can help you pay for the costs of long-term care. Include as part of your plan an implementation schedule. Give yourself deadlines to accomplish each of the necessary steps to put your plan into action.

The final step is to review the plan periodically. Don't forget, financial planning is a process. It is ongoing and constantly changing. Not only can your circumstances change, but tax and other laws are also ever changing. Your goal will become a moving target. Your only hope of hitting it is to review your strategies at least once a year and to make changes as needed.

5

THE RISK MANAGEMENT PROCESS

Planning for long-term care is an exercise in risk management. Risk management is also a *process,* not an event. As a process, risk management involves monitoring your exposure to risk and the techniques you are using to cope with it. Risk management is ongoing, with periodic reviews and adjustments essential to success.

Risk management is a three-step process. The first step is to identify, analyze, and quantify the risks you face. Next, you should select from among the available risk management techniques those that seem most appropriate for your situation. Finally, you must periodically review your situation and modify or replace the risk management techniques you are using.

The risk of long-term care can be expressed in both financial and emotional terms. Financial costs of long-term care can be devastating. Even an average stay in a nursing home for custodial care can wipe out the accumulated wealth of a lifetime for some people. If the children, grandchildren, or other family members are sharing the financial burden, long-term care costs can strain their finances beyond the breaking point.

Emotional costs can be just as devastating as financial ones. The elderly person must cope with the inability to do once easy things. After 70 or more years of being self-reliant, it is a tremendous adjustment to depend on someone else for something as simple as dressing. Older persons may begin to think of themselves as a burden on their families. Younger family members must cope not only with the trials of raising children but the needs

17

of an aging parent. They may invest so much time, energy, and emotional capital that they may think they have nothing left for themselves or their spouse.

When assessing and analyzing a risk, you must look not only at the absolute size of the risk but also its relative size. For example, assume that local nursing home costs are $30,000 per year. If your net worth, other than your home, is $100,000, spending a couple of years or more in a nursing home will seriously deplete the accumulated wealth of a lifetime. On the other hand, if your net worth is $1 million or more, most reasonably foreseeable stays in a nursing home will not seriously threaten to wipe you out.

As a very rough guide, the financial risk of long-term custodial care is probably greatest for people with assets (other than their home) of more than $100,000 and under $1 million. Those at the lower end of the spectrum may already come close to qualifying for government aid under the Medicaid program (See Key 18). Those at the upper end may be able to fund an expected nursing home stay on their investment earnings alone. Those in the middle face the greatest risk to their wealth.

Once the risk has been identified, the next step is to select appropriate risk management techniques. Risk management is not an exotic idea that requires complex strategies. As you will see, risk management is really just common sense that is rigorously applied. There are five basic risk management techniques:

1. Avoid the risk
2. Reduce the exposure to risk
3. Reduce the size of the potential loss
4. Shift the risk
5. Accept the risk

Avoiding risk is a simple concept that is often difficult to apply. It's very easy to avoid the risk of dying in a shipwreck if you never take a cruise. It is far more difficult to avoid the risk of a traffic accident because virtually everyone in our society must at least occasionally use the roadways. Long-term care most often arises out of the maladies associated with aging. Since you can't avoid aging, you can't totally avoid the risk that you may someday require custodial care.

A more common technique is to reduce the risk that a damaging act or event will occur. Smart pedestrians want to reduce the chance that they will be hit by a car, so they cross the street only in designated crosswalks with a green light. Manufacturers place guards and other devices on production equipment to reduce the chance of injuries. To some extent, the medical conditions that give rise to the need for long-term care can be prevented. A healthy diet, plenty of exercise, and regular check-ups with your doctor can reduce the risk that you will need long-term care. Other conditions, however, may be hereditary, may strike randomly, or may not be preventable through lifestyle changes. Thus, you probably won't be able to eliminate the risk of long-term care using this technique.

You can also manage risk by reducing the size of the loss you will suffer if a loss occurs. Seat belts, for example, do not reduce the risk of having a collision; however, they do reduce the chance that you will be seriously injured. There are steps, as you will see, that you can take to reduce the cost—both financial and emotional—of long-term care. For example, you may be able to avail yourself of some of the tax benefits discussed in Keys 35 to 44. With respect to the emotional costs, becoming familiar with "respite care" (Key 13), and "home health care" (Key 12) may serve to ease some of the burden.

Transferring the risk to a third party is another very useful option. The most common example of transferring risk is an insurance policy. We are all familiar with common types of insurance such as automobile, home-owner's, life, and health insurance. A new breed of insurance policy has developed recently to deal specifically with the problem of long-term care. Your insurance options will be discussed in detail in Keys 20 to 25.

The final technique of risk management is to accept the risk. We accept risks every day. We drive cars and fly in airplanes despite the possibility of a crash. However, if you decide to accept risk, accept it knowingly. Hiding from the risk of long-term care or pretending that it will never happen is no solution. In fact, it is a prescription for disaster. A wiser decision is to adopt a position such as: "I am willing to risk up to 25 percent of my net worth on long-term care" or "I am willing to risk that I will have to pay nursing home bills for up to three months." The key is to accept *calculated* risks.

The final step in the risk management process is to regularly review and adjust your strategies. That may involve more frequent check-ups to catch little problems before they become big ones. Or, it might involve moving closer to a child or grandchild who will provide care if it is required. Finally, it might involve reviewing a new generation of long-term care insurance policies to see if any improvements better meet your needs.

6

ASSEMBLING YOUR TEAM OF ADVISORS

Planning for long-term care needs requires a multitude of skills. The problem involves medical, legal, tax, insurance, financial, and other areas. If you have the time, interest, and talent, you can, through diligent study, probably acquire the knowledge to do much of the work yourself. Many, however, will be unwilling to pay the high price of lost time and expended energy to learn to do it all themselves. In any case, many medical, legal, and tax matters are sufficiently complex so that prudent persons will leave at least those aspects to highly trained specialists.

Because financial planning is an interdisciplinary process, it makes sense to assemble a team of advisors. It is doubtful that any one individual possesses all the required skills and training to help you meet your objective. The financial planning process, as it applies to personal financial matters, is very similar to the planning process used by businesses to plan for their growth and survival. Because you are in charge of your financial affairs, doesn't it make sense to approach them in the same way that the president of a large corporation approaches planning?

As the person most responsible for your own financial future, you may want to do what the presidents of many businesses do—hire someone to be your "vice president of finance." This is the person to whom you look first for financial advice. Your vice president of finance may be your accountant or your attorney. Many people employ financial planners to act as their chief financial advisors. They turn to their accountant, attorney, insurance agent, stockbroker, or other advisors for specialized advice.

Ideally, financial planners have broad training and experience in personal financial matters. Your financial planner should also be experienced in advising clients about long-term care matters. Unfortunately, it is far too easy for anyone to use the term *financial planner* without having the required amount of knowledge, experience, and integrity.

Financial planners today come in all shapes, sizes, and packages. Some attorneys and accountants offer personal financial planning services. Some insurance agents call themselves planners, as do some who are employed by investment, financial services and brokerage companies. Four critical issues must be addressed when selecting a financial planner:

• Knowledge
• Experience
• Integrity
• Compensation

Exploring these four issues requires some investigative work on your part. The best way to find out about a planner is to ask questions. Ask the planner about former or current clients and any applicable regulatory body. Financial planners are subject to a patchwork of regulation. You may have to contact the state or local bar association or the state board regulating Certified Public Accountants. You may also need to check with your state's insurance commissioner or securities commissioner. The federal Securities and Exchange Commission may also be a potential source of information. Finally, you may be able to gather information from your local Better Business Bureau.

It is important to know, up front, how your planner will be compensated and, to the extent that an estimate is possible, how much the service will cost. Financial planners generally use one of three compensation methods. Some planners charge a flat fee for their services. These fee-only planners generally include most accountants and lawyers who offer planning services as well as those who are just financial planners. Fee-only planners tend to cater to the needs of wealthy people. Other financial planners charge both a fee and earn commissions if you choose to purchase insurance or other financial products and services from them. Still other planners are compensated only if you purchase some type of product from them.

Determining what a planner knows or does not know can be difficult. One indication may be the professional designations your planner has achieved. These designations are evidenced by a series of initials after his or her name. CFPs or Certified Financial Planners have completed a course of training (usually 18 months to two years) offered by the College for Financial Planning or other approved educational institution. CLUs are Chartered Life Underwriters. These individuals tend to be insurance professionals and have passed a series of courses on financial planning, with an emphasis on insurance, offered by the American College. ChFCs or chartered financial consultants are also most often insurance professionals, and they have completed another course, focused more on financial planning, offered by the American College. Lawyers may have a variety of professional degrees. JD and LLB are the two standard abbreviations for law degrees. LLM indicates that the attorney has completed a master's program. Many lawyers who practice in the area of personal financial planning have an LLM in taxation. Accountants in private practice are usually CPAs or certified public accountants. This designation is awarded after completing college; passing a comprehensive test on accounting, business law, and auditing; and, in most states, having a certain level of experience. Some accountants also have the designation APFS, which stands for accredited personal financial specialist. These CPAs have passed a further examination covering personal financial planning matters and administered by the American Institute of CPAs.

Although professional designations are an indication of expertise, they are not a guarantee. A CPA is not necessarily familiar with Medicaid. A law degree does not make one an expert in insurance. Your investigation into your vice president of finance's actual experience, therefore, is important. Some graduates of the college of hard knocks are as capable of providing good advice as those with a series of professional designations.

Your advisor's experience is also important. Ask your advisor how long he or she has been providing advice in this area. Although it would be nice to find someone with 25 years of experience, the area of long-term care planning is fairly new. Experience in related financial planning matters, however, may be a good guide. Some of the most experienced financial planners are members of the Registry of Financial Planning Practitioners sponsored by the International Association for Financial Planning.

Your planner's integrity is also critical. Honesty and fairness in business practices and objectivity are important factors. The method of compensating your planner may influence some planners. If your planner is being paid solely through commissions, a natural conflict of interest is created. If you don't buy, the planner doesn't get paid. This conflict can and does influence some commission-earning planners. However, many planners who earn commissions successfully manage this conflict every day. They are honorable sales professionals who recognize that some people won't need their services and won't sell to those who don't. These planners value their reputation, long-term staying power in the profession, and your potential to refer others who might be better suited to their service. The method of compensation is certainly a relevant issue. It is not, however, the only consideration. Consider also the individual's manner, reputation, and recommendations from existing clients as well as the method of compensation.

Finding your way through the maze of problems and pitfalls involved in the area of long-term care is best accomplished with a team of competent advisors. Your doctor, lawyer, and other advisors will be critical members of the team. But someone needs to lead the effort, develop overall strategies, and coordinate their implementation. Although you will always have the final say in whatever steps need to be taken, a financial planner may be just the type of individual you can turn to as your vice president of finance.

7

WHERE TO GET HELP—
AN OVERVIEW

Planning for long-term care requires that you know where you can turn for help should the need arise. Your needs may involve bringing someone—a friend, relative, or a professional care provider—into your home to provide the help you need. You may need to consider various other housing options. In addition to securing the care you need, you may also need help coping with the emotional, financial, bureaucratic, and legal aspects of long-term care. Keys 8 through 14 provide you with some guidance about your alternatives when you are seeking help.

Housing is a particular concern for people facing long-term care. Most senior citizens want to remain as independent as possible for as long as possible. Familiar surroundings and the ability to visit with family and friends are also important. The senior citizen also wants a sense of security in his or her home. The housing structure should not hinder the effective and efficient delivery of health care.

When some people think of long-term care, they think only of nursing homes. Nursing homes (discussed in Key 8) are certainly a common solution. They are not, however, the only option. Many seniors are able to receive the level of care they need in their own home (See Key 12). Others move in with their children or other relatives. Keys 11 and 12 touch on some of the issues involved in that decision. Sometimes, staying in your own home or in the home of a relative isn't possible. Before opting for a nursing home, consider several other options. You might select one of the shared living arrangements discussed in Key 10. You might also consider the possibility of living in the continuing care retirement communities discussed in Key 9.

The problems faced by the elderly are handled by a wide range of federal, state, and local government agencies, as well as by numerous private charities, agencies, and associations. These various groups may be able to provide the help you need or assist you in securing the help you need. Some may also provide you with a forum to resolve a problem or complaint with a care provider. The names, addresses, and telephone numbers of many of these agencies are listed in the Appendix.

8

NURSING HOMES

Nursing homes are designed to provide long-term custodial care and medical services that are less intensive than a hospital. For years they have been viewed as the principal source of long-term care services outside of the home. As you will see in Keys 8 through 14 there are a number of alternatives to nursing homes today.

The move into a nursing home is rarely an easy one. For some, the nursing home will be only a temporary stop on the road to recovery; for many others, the nursing home will be their last home. For some, a nursing home may be one of several alternatives; for others, it may be the only alternative. As pointed out in Key 3, nursing homes are frightfully expensive. Given their critical importance, it pays to understand as much as possible about them.

Nursing homes are generally divided into three levels of care, Skilled Nursing Facilities (SNF), Intermediate Care Facilities (ICF), and Residential Care Facilities (RCF). An RCF is also called a custodial care nursing home. In some cases, the entire nursing home may be devoted to one level of care or another. Other nursing homes offer more than one level of care in different parts of the facility.

The levels of care are distinguished by the frequency and the complexity of the nursing services offered. The federal regulations that spell out the differences are, like most regulations, more than a little complex. Essentially, the more care that is required and the more skilled the person administering the care, the higher the level of care will be. Skilled nursing care requires, among other things, that you receive 24-hour care from a registered nurse. Intermediate care is a less intensive level of care. In an ICF you may receive care from a registered nurse, but it will not be required on a 24-hour basis. In a custodial care facility, your care generally consists of assistance with the activities of daily life (ADL). This care is often provided by licensed practical nurses and nursing assistants who have received less training than registered nurses. ADLs are simple, basic activities such as eating, bathing, dressing, transferring (getting in and out of a bed or a chair), walking, and toileting. The concept of ADLs is also important within the context of some long-term care insurance policies (See Key 23).

Custodial care is the crux of the problem of planning for long-term care. It tends to last the longest and is quite expensive (See Key 3). Medicare does not cover it (See Key 16). Medicaid will cover it, but Medicaid is a program for the poor (See Key 18). Nevertheless, many people cannot live without this type of care.

Medicare and Medicaid authorities must approve of a nursing facility before they will make a payment to the facility. Not all nursing facilities are Medicare and Medicaid approved. Any facility receiving federal funds must adhere to a uniform set of rules, a "bill of rights" for nursing home patients. These rights include many fundamental freedoms such as the freedom to choose a personal doctor. The resident also has a right to privacy and a right to be free from abuse of any kind. Restraints may be used only to protect the patient and other residents and then only by specific written order of a doctor. Also included is the right to have an accounting of all personal funds held by the home. These and the other rights must be communicated to the resident when he or she is admitted.

Choosing a nursing home can be a particularly difficult task. Part of the difficulty can be attributed to psychological factors. The older person may be depressed by the thought of entering an institution. The family of the older person may feel a sense of failure because they can no longer provide care. Because the decision to enter a nursing home is not often viewed positively, it is difficult for the decision makers to feel upbeat and enthusiastic about their task. Add to this the wide range of quality and services provided by nursing homes and you have the makings of a difficult decision.

Three critical factors must be considered when selecting a nursing home: the quality and nature of its services, the cost of its services and the forms of payment it will accept, and the proximity to friends and family. Quality is an elusive concept that is difficult to apply, particularly in the case of nursing homes. Is a quality nursing home one that has large common areas, expensive furniture, and well-kept grounds? Or is a home that has less grand appointments, but a friendly, courteous staff and a creative Activities Director a better bet? It is probably best to consider comfortable surroundings, high-quality food, cleanliness, a friendly and supportive staff, activities, rehabilitative services, and good health care as indications of quality.

The nature of the services is also important. You will want to find a home that can provide for current needs. However, because elderly people find relocating to be particularly difficult, it may be wise to find a home that can provide a higher level of care if needed.

Nursing homes costs vary widely (See Key 3). Some nursing homes are run as a for-profit enterprise, whereas others are run by churches and other nonprofit organizations. It is possible to spend a great deal more money without improving the quality of service, so it pays to visit several homes. Some nursing homes will not accept Medicare or Medicaid residents or may display favoritism towards private pay (i.e., non-Medicaid) residents, even though such discrimination against Medicaid patients by homes accepting federal aid is prohibited. A lack of participation in Medicaid is not necessarily an indicator of quality. Some very fine homes have simply chosen not to accept Medicaid payments. Because Medicaid is a realistic possibility for anyone in the middle class (e.g., between $100,000 to $1,000,000 in assets excluding the home) who has not planned properly, it's important to learn the methods of payment the home will accept.

Having a home that is accessible to family and friends is very important. People in nursing homes can be very lonely and may feel abandoned by loved ones. Having a home close by so that family and friends can visit can bring joy into the lives of nursing home residents and can also enrich the lives of the family and friends who visit.

The Appendix lists agencies that can provide further information about choosing the most appropriate nursing home for your needs.

9

CONTINUING CARE RETIREMENT COMMUNITIES

The ideal retirement home for many senior citizens is a home in which they can maintain their independence and privacy, live near people with similar interests, have security, and have an increasing level of care as their health requires. Such a retirement home is not a pipe dream; it exists today. It is often called a continuing care retirement community (CCRC). Continuing care retirement communities are similar to life-care communities.

CCRCs are gaining popularity. There are wide variations among the types of services provided, the quality of those services, and their cost. However, all CCRCs have certain characteristics in common. First, there is generally a substantial (sometimes in excess of $100,000) fee that is charged upon entry into the community. This fee is sometimes called an entrance fee or an endowment. In addition, a monthly fee is charged. In exchange for the fee, the community agrees to provide an apartment, cottage, or other dwelling place and certain other specified services and amenities (for example, some meals, laundry services, transportation, cleaning, and the like). The community also promises to provide you with increasing levels of personal care in the event you require custodial or skilled nursing care.

For many senior citizens, these communities are indeed an ideal solution to their housing needs. CCRCs are particularly appropriate for the more affluent who can afford the sometimes substantial entrance fee. Senior citizens who want to rid themselves of the work involved in maintaining a private home can use the proceeds from the sale of their home to pay the entrance fee. The sale of the home may involve a substantial gain for tax purposes. The special tax treatment of home sales is discussed in Key 40. A portion of the entrance fee may be attributable to medical services. That portion of the fee may be deductible for income tax purposes. For a discussion of the deductibility of medical expenses see Key 35.

CCRCs can provide a much wanted sense of security. The facility may be equipped with alarms and other systems to deter burglars and other criminals. Some facilities also have medical alert systems to bring help to a resident who has fallen or is otherwise in need. One of the biggest advantages of a CCRC is that the residents have access to nursing home care should the need arise. The nursing home care in some CCRCs may be unlimited in length and at no additional charge over the normal monthly fee. Other facilities may put a limit on the length of time the standard fee will cover nursing services. Because moving out of the home and into a nursing facility can be one of the most difficult decisions an elderly person faces, it can be very comforting to have the nursing facility in or near very familiar surroundings.

CCRCs also have their disadvantages. The first and most obvious is the cost. The entrance fee plus the monthly fee can be quite substantial. In addition, the entrance fee is generally nonrefundable, regardless of how long you live in the home. The level of services also varies from CCRC to CCRC. Some CCRCs offer an all-inclusive service under which all community services are covered under one fee. Others may have some services available, for example custodial care nursing services, but may charge an additional fee if they are used. Entering a CCRC generally requires that you sign a contract. These contracts, like any other legal document, should be reviewed carefully. If you don't feel comfortable reviewing the contract yourself, you may want to consult an attorney. Finally, because the relationship with the CCRC is a contractual relationship, you must consider the CCRC's ability to fulfill its end of the bargain. The CCRC may promise that it will provide nursing home services if you need them, but what happens if the facility is experiencing financial difficulties just when you need help? CCRCs are sponsored by both profit and nonprofit organizations. The quality of the community's finances may be just as important as the quality of its services.

CCRCs can be found in most parts of the country, although they are particularly popular in certain regions particularly east of the Mississippi. To find out more about these communities, contact the Continuing Care Accreditation Commission, 1129 Twentieth Street N.W., Suite 400, Washington, D.C. 20036. The telephone number is (202) 296-5960.

10

SHARED LIVING ARRANGEMENTS

Sharing a home may be a viable option for many seniors who need help managing a home, who can't get that help from relatives, and who want to remain outside of a nursing home or other more institutional setting for as long as possible. Shared living arrangements take on a variety of forms. The arrangement may simply involve having a renter move into your home or you moving into the home of another. The home may be shared by a larger group. You may also be able to find a group arrangement that provides services in addition to housing and help with household chores. This Key explores some of the options available for shared living arrangements.

The simplest shared living arrangement involves having someone move into your home as a boarder. In exchange for the living space, the boarder pays rent and may provide help in maintaining the home, running errands, and other minor chores. A variation of this same idea involves you becoming the boarder at someone else's home. Some communities even have adult foster care programs, which function the same as the foster care programs for children.

For those who need only a little extra help, shared living is a viable alternative. It may be a low-cost way to maintain your independence, presence in the community, and social contacts, while providing you with the help you need. There are also some obvious disadvantages. First, local zoning and other land use rules may prohibit two unrelated people from using a single family home as a two-family home. You must also select your boarder or landlord very carefully. There are numerous issues related to the rights and responsibilities of the two parties sharing the home. The Shared Housing Resource Center (their address and phone number are listed in the Appendix) may be able to provide you with further information if you decide to pursue a home sharing arrangement.

An extension of the home sharing concept is the group home or group shared residence. This form of shared living involves a small (about four) to medium sized (15 to 20) group of people sharing a home, small apartment building, or other living facility. The home may be sponsored by a charitable or other nonprofit organization. The residents of the home may share responsibility for managing the home, the sponsoring organization may take some or all of that responsibility, or the group members may hire housekeepers and others to perform those jobs. Assembling or finding a compatible group may be challenging. And there are legal hurdles to be overcome when creating group homes. Group homes, however, do present a viable alternative for some senior citizens.

Congregate housing is another variation of the shared living concept. In a congregate living center or community, senior citizens, who otherwise might be living independently, live in an apartment-type building. Some meal services, linen services, housekeeping, or other hotel-like services are generally provided as part of a package of services. Many of these communities were created using federal funds and they cater to lower income seniors. Private developers have also developed more upscale versions of congregate housing.

The board and care home is another potential alternative for seniors who require some help in coping with the activities of daily life, but who still desire and are able to live among a small group of people. Board and care homes, assisted living, shelter care, domiciliary care, and residential care all refer to similar housing activities.

A board and care home involves a small group of people living together in a home or small apartment building. Typically, the owner of the home runs the board and care facility with the hope of turning a profit. The owner of the home may have simply converted his or her existing home into a board and care home by renting out rooms. Sometimes these homes are operated by charitable organizations. In exchange for a month's rent, the residents are generally entitled to a room and meals. Cleaning services, laundry services, and other services may also be included. The home may or may not have to be licensed, depending on state and local laws.

The residents of a board and care home tend to be able to participate in the activities of daily life such as toileting, dressing, and eating. The home, however, does provide them with an opportunity for social interaction. They also may have more independence and freedom of movement then would be possible in a nursing home. The residents generally share living, kitchen, dining, and bathroom facilities. Their bedroom may be shared as well, depending on the home.

There are many advantages to board and care homes. They create a homey environment while still providing some assistance to the elderly person. They generally lack the institutional restrictions of a nursing home. Loneliness is a common problem among elderly people, and board and care homes, like other shared living arrangements, provide a ready made group of people with whom life can be shared. Board and care homes also are generally quite cost effective.

There are, of course, disadvantages as well. Because board and care homes are not uniformly regulated, some homes may be poorly run, and you may have fewer remedies if you encounter problems. There is also the possibility that you simply may not like the group of people who share the home. Living in close proximity to a small group of people can lead to problems if some members of the group just don't like each other.

As a tenant, you are also subject to the usual risks faced by tenants. If the financial situation of your landlord deteriorates, the services you are used to may be reduced or eliminated. If the home is mortgaged, a foreclosure is a possibility if the debt becomes unmanageable. You may also be forced to move should your condition require a higher level of care than the home can provide. Finally, some homes may have architectural barriers that may prevent the use of wheelchairs or other devices. These barriers may limit your choices among different homes, or they may force you to leave a home if a wheelchair is later required.

11

ECHO UNITS

ECHO stands for elder cottage housing opportunity. The acronym may be new, but the concept has been around for many years. Most elderly people would prefer home care to institutional care. If their health or some other reason prevents them from living in their own homes, their children may offer to allow them to move into their home. One compromise to preserve some semblance of independence for the parent while allowing the child the access necessary to provide the care needed is the ECHO unit.

The ECHO concept started several years ago in Australia. ECHO housing generally refers to the creation of a new, temporary housing structure on the site (and, perhaps, attached to) the existing house. The elderly person occupies the ECHO, while the family of the adult child occupies the main house. In this country in many, mostly rural, areas, the notion of providing housing by using buildings either close to or attached to the main house has been around for years. In more urban areas, mother-in-law suites, mother-in-law flats, or accessory apartments are quite common. These flats or suites generally consist of converting unused space into an apartment for the elderly person. All of these housing units are designed to provide the elderly with a sense of independence, without removing them too far from those who provide daily care.

Each of these ancillary structures has its own bedroom and bath. In addition, the new unit may have its own kitchen, dining area, living area, and entrance. In some cases, the changes to the existing home are relatively minor. In other cases, constructing the ECHO unit may involve substantial changes to the home, lot, or both.

A variety of questions must be addressed when considering an ECHO or other similar addition. Among the first questions you should ask is whether there are any zoning, housing code, deed restrictions, or other legal impediments to constructing the planned unit. In some areas the conversion of a single-family home into a two-family home or one lot with two homes conflicts with local housing laws. Next, you should decide how elaborate your unit will be. You should take to heart the financial considerations of constructing such a unit when evaluating your options. When deciding on the layout of your addition and the budget within which you must work, you may want to retain a professional architect or a home remodeling contractor with access to an architect. Once you have decided on your basic needs, you may then begin to consult remodeling contractors and/or general contractors to solicit bids for the project. The very energetic and skilled among you may want to save on construction costs and do some or all of the work on your own.

The addition of an ECHO may satisfy the needs of the adult children to know that their elderly parents are safe and well cared for while giving the aged parent a continued sense of independence. However, ECHO units should not be constructed without careful consideration of the legal restrictions, construction costs, and financing expenses.

12

HOME CARE

Most senior citizens requiring long-term care would prefer to receive their care in a homelike setting. Nursing homes and other institutions, regardless of the quality of the care and the surroundings, just aren't the same in the eyes of many. The first choice is generally the senior citizen's own home. A secondary choice may be the home of a child or other loved one.

Will home care make sense for you? That depends entirely on your circumstances. Perhaps the overriding consideration is the state of your health. The more care you require, the more difficult home care will be. Another factor is the availability of help. Help can come in many forms. For married senior citizens, a healthy spouse will probably be a principal care giver. For single seniors, or those whose spouses are also in ill health, the proximity of family and friends and their ability to provide help become important considerations. Finally, the resources of government agencies, charitable groups, and for profit enterprises in your area will be helpful in filling the gaps in the services and level of care that can be performed by family and friends.

A frank discussion with your doctor may be the place to start when deciding whether home care is appropriate. The family's ability to absorb the care of an elderly member must also be considered. Geographic proximity, the constraints of caring for children and other immediate family members, care giving skills, travel and other career-related restrictions, and a host of other factors may reduce family members' ability to provide adequate care.

Your community may provide a wealth of resources to make home care possible. One way to determine the types of services available in your area is to start with your state office on aging. Every state has a department devoted to dealing with the services available to the elderly. The Appendix contains a listing of these state agencies. You will be able to learn the location and telephone number of your Area Agency on Aging from the statewide central office. Some of the services available may be free or have only a nominal cost. Other services will have fees, some of which could be substantial. For the most part, these community-based home care services are probably not covered by Medicare (See Keys 16 and 17).

Some resources in your community may be mandated by law. For example, many municipalities offer elderly homeowners various ways to lower their property tax bill. The tax relief may include a credit against the tax, the ability to defer the tax, or a freeze in the value of the home against which the tax is assessed. The tax relief may be available to any senior citizen or there may be income or other limitations. In addition, some areas control the rents that may be charged senior citizens in some cases. Finally, some utility companies, either as a business practice or as a result of legislation, may offer some relief from high utility bills. You may qualify for some type of government aid to pay utility bills, or the utility company may offer some form of deferred billing or other benefit to help make these expenses more manageable.

A wide variety of services may be available in your community. Churches, community groups and other charities provide hot meal programs, housekeeping services, shopping assistance, and volunteers for home repairs and maintenance, among other things. The Red Cross offers educational programs and certain other services. Community mental health agencies and other health care groups can provide counseling for both the elderly person and the care giver. Of course, for-profit visiting nurses, housekeepers, and other service providers are also available for their respective fees. The list of possible support groups seems endless. Armed with information provided by your Area Agency on Aging and your local telephone directory, you should be able to determine the types of services available to you.

13

HELP FOR THE CARE GIVER

Tending to the needs of a frail, elderly person is hard work. It is especially hard if you are simultaneously trying to raise a growing family. Single parents helping to care for an elderly relative face a particularly daunting task. Help is available in a variety of forms.

Care givers may need help in two different ways. First, if the care givers work outside the home and an elderly person requiring care lives with them, a regular system of providing help during working hours is needed. Care givers who do not work outside the home need to take periodic breaks from the constant demands placed upon them. Respite care is available in various forms to provide the care giver the time to tend to personal business or just relax.

Many communities have multipurpose senior centers. These centers provide a social gathering place. They also provide cultural, recreational, and educational programs. Senior centers tend to cater to the needs of healthy, independent seniors, although programs for those requiring a greater degree of care are also available. Centers may also offer limited health care services such as high blood pressure screening. Transportation to and from the center and elsewhere may be provided. The programs at these centers vary considerably and many communities have several different senior center programs. So, it pays to investigate all the centers that operate in your area. Your telephone directory and Area Agency on Aging may be able to help you find a center suited to your needs.

For seniors who require more care, adult day care centers are becoming more and more popular. These centers operate similarly to centers for children. They may be used by care givers who work outside the home as well as by at-home care givers who need a break. Adult day care centers are generally able to handle the needs of elderly people who require a greater degree of care. The centers offer recreational, artistic, cultural, and other programs for their senior citizen patrons. Meals are also generally included. Some of these centers may accept Medicaid payments.

Care givers often benefit from sharing their feelings and frustrations. Care giver support groups have grown in popularity in recent years. These groups give those providing long-term care to an elderly relative a chance to share ideas and experiences with others. You can locate a local support group through your Area Agency on Aging. The National Council on Aging has also published a directory called the *Idea Book On Care-giver Support Groups*. The address and telephone number can be found in the Appendix.

In some instances, the elderly person cannot practically leave the care giver's home. In these cases, substitutes must be brought in to provide the care giver with a break from responsibilities. Visiting nurses and housekeeping services are often used by elderly people who are staying in their own homes. These same services can be used by the care giver when they need to get away for awhile. Your Area Agency on Aging will be able to help you locate these services in your area.

14

HOSPICE

One special type of long-term care program is directed toward the needs of the terminally ill. Hospice programs exist across the country to provide aid and comfort to the terminally ill and their families. Over 1,400 hospice programs across the country currently meet the needs of over 200,000 patients.

The hospice movement began in the late 1960s in England and spread to this country about 1974. Hospice is as much a philosophy of treatment as it is a physical place. Hospice is often associated with needs of cancer victims; however, all terminally ill people, regardless of the nature of their disease, should have access to a local program. Hospice programs may be associated with a hospital, nursing home, or other health care facility. There may be in-patient facilities for patients who are not receiving care at home, but home care is also an integral part of a hospice program.

Hospice programs are designed to provide the terminally ill with care designed to relieve pain, whether physical, emotional, spiritual, or financial. Hospice patients have been diagnosed as having only a few weeks or months to live. The patient is no longer receiving care or treatment intended to cure the illness. Rather, at a hospice the patient receives care designed to minimize the symptoms of the disease.

Hospice programs are designed to provide comfort and counseling to both the patient and family. Some hospice programs are intended to provide a respite to at-home care givers by providing a place for the terminally ill patient to receive care while the care givers take a short, well-deserved break. Counseling and other services are available both to the patient and family.

The personnel at a hospice will be interdisciplinary. Doctors and nurses are integral parts of a hospice team. The patient's personal physician has probably referred the patient to the hospice and may continue to play an active role in treatment. The hospice team also includes social workers who can provide counseling services on a variety of topics, including the financial aspects of care and the use of community and governmental resources. Members of the clergy are also part of a hospice program. Many of those providing services at hospices are volunteers. All hospice workers undergo extensive screening and training.

Medicare provides hospice benefits. Medicare Part A provides a total of 210 days of hospice care as well as benefits for some drug treatments. (See Key 16 for more details.) Hospice care is also among the benefits that the states can offer Medicaid recipients.

15

PAYING FOR LONG-TERM CARE

As we have seen, long-term custodial care is enormously expensive. There are only four possible ways to pay these costs: out of your pocket, out of your family's pocket, out of the government's pocket, and out of an insurance company's pocket. To the extent that you can shift the burden to the government or to an insurance company, you reduce the chance that either you or your family will be financially wiped out by long-term care expenses.

Some surveys have suggested that we are woefully unprepared to meet long-term expenses. One recent survey suggests that 22 percent of those surveyed believe that long-term care bills will come from savings. Other statistics, however, indicate that many people only have enough savings to cover a few months of care. About 15 percent of those surveyed believe that insurance policies will pay the bill. As you will see in Key 20, private health insurance, including Medicare supplement or Medigap policies, generally do not cover long-term custodial care. Relatively few people have taken the step to purchase insurance specifically designed to meet long-term care needs, although it is one of the fastest growing types of insurance (See Keys 21 through 24). About 10 percent believe that Medicare or Social Security will pay the bills. Keys 16 and 17 make it clear that Medicare is not the answer. About 11 percent of those surveyed indicate that they expect to pay out of their pocket for an elderly relative. These people are fairly realistic in their expectations, although they may not realize just how expensive long-term care really is. Only two percent of those surveyed thought that Medicaid (or other welfare programs) will pay. Sadly, Medicaid pays almost half of all long-term care bills. Medicaid, as is explained in Keys 18 and 19, is a welfare program for poor people. About 10 percent of those surveyed thought this money was going to come from an unidentified source (the lottery?). Perhaps the most disturbing statistic is that 30 percent simply had no idea how they would pay for long-term care expenses.

There is no simple answer to the problem. For most people, paying for long-term care needs will be a combination of their own resources, their family's resources, the government's resources, and insurance resources. To create the proper mix, you will need to understand some of the existing government and insurance options. The next 10 Keys and the Appendix explore these options.

16

MEDICARE PART A

Many people assume that Medicare will cover long-term care expenses. Nothing could be further from the truth. In fact, on average, Medicare only pays about two percent of long-term care expenses. Congress attempted to provide at least some measure of protection under the Medicare Catastrophic Care Act. Unfortunately, this much maligned law missed the mark, both on the type of benefits provided and on the funding mechanism. Funding was to have been supplied by a surtax on Medicare recipients. Facing a near revolt by the elderly, Congress repealed most of the Medicare Catastrophic Act in 1989. Today, we are left with a national health care system that is not designed to cover most of the long-term care needs of the elderly and younger disabled population.

In spite of the inadequacies of the Medicare system, it is useful to review some of the benefits it provides for long-term care. Medicare is divided into two parts, A and B. Part A is also called the Basic Hospital Insurance Plan. This component of Medicare is automatically available, at no additional charge, to anyone over 65 who receives Social Security retirement benefits. Those over 65, but not covered by Social Security, may be able to obtain Part A coverage by applying for it and paying a monthly premium, provided they are also covered by Medicare Part B.

Medicare is a federal program administered by the Health Care Financing Administration. Part A is almost entirely funded by taxes collected by the federal government. Medicare will only pay for health care services provided by an approved facility. For long-term care purposes, an approved facility can include a hospital, skilled nursing facility, home health care agency, or hospice.

In a hospital, Medicare Part A covers such services as the following:

- bed and board in a semiprivate room
- operating room charges
- nursing services (other than private duty nurses)
- diagnostic and therapeutic items
- various other items associated with hospital bills

However, Part A will *not* cover doctors' bills and nonmedical items requested by the patient for personal comfort (i.e., a radio or television). The Medicare hospital benefit is subject to limitations and deductibles and coinsurance features.

In each "benefit period," Medicare Part A pays for up to 90 days of hospital care. A *benefit period* (or spell of illness) is defined as the period that begins on the first day of hospitalization and ends 60 days after discharge. For example, Ralph, age 66, enters the hospital on June 3 and is discharged on June 27. Ralph's benefits period starts June 3 and will end (provided he doesn't require further treatment covered under Part A) in 60 days, on August 26.

For the first 60 days of hospitalization, the patient must pay (in 1991) a deductible of $628. From day 61 to day 90, the patient pays a coinsurance amount of $157 (in 1991) per day. After 90 days, everyone is allowed a 60-day lifetime reserve of coverage. The coinsurance amount for this period (in 1991) is $314 per day. Beyond 150 days of hospitalization, the patient pays 100 percent of the cost.

Medicare also covers certain confinements in skilled nursing facilities. Do not be lulled into a sense of complacency by this coverage. This coverage has numerous restrictions, and it is not available at all if you require custodial rather than skilled nursing services. Essentially, skilled nursing care means that you are under a doctor's care, and the services you are receiving can only be provided by or under the supervision of a licensed nurse. You must require these skilled services on a daily basis. Generally, you must be admitted to the skilled nursing facility after a three-day hospital stay and within 30 days of your release from the hospital. Of course, the skilled nursing home must be Medicare approved.

Assuming all the prerequisites are met, Medicare Part A will pay each benefit period for up to 100 days of care in a skilled nursing facility. For the first 20 days, Medicare pays 100 percent of the approved amount (Medicare will not pay more than the amount allowable under its rules). For the next 80 days, Medicare pays 100 percent of the cost in excess of $78.50 per day. This amount is adjusted annually. Beyond 100 days, Medicare provides no benefits. However, every time you begin a new benefit period, you may have another 100-day period of coverage.

Medicare also pays for some post-hospital home health services. Four conditions must be met for coverage:

- The care must be skilled nursing, physical therapy, or speech therapy provided on an intermittent (not more than five days per week) basis.
- The patient must be homebound or confined. You are confined to your home if your condition restricts your ability to leave home without the assistance of another person or some device (i.e., walker or wheelchair).
- The home care must be part of a course of treatment established by a doctor.
- Services must be provided by a Medicare-approved

home health care agency, and Medicare will only pay the approved amount.

If these prerequisites are met, Medicare Part A will pay for the full cost, up to approved amounts, for as many visits as are medically necessary. Medicare only pays for 80 percent of the cost of durable medical equipment such as wheelchairs. Note, however, that the services must be skilled nursing services. Help with bathing, dressing, cooking, cleaning, and other custodial services are *not* covered.

Medicare Part A also provides hospice benefits. The coverage will be provided to terminally ill patients diagnosed as having six months or less to live. Medicare provides two 90-day benefit periods and one 30-day benefit period. Generally, Medicare will pay all costs for the hospice stay within these periods. Naturally, Medicare payments are further limited to what it computes as reasonable. In addition, there is a five percent (up to $5) coinsurance amount for drugs. Finally, there are respite care benefits available for up to five days with a five percent coinsurance feature. Respite care involves taking a terminally ill individual who is currently being cared for in a home into the hospice for a short period of time to give his or her at-home care givers relief from the rigors of constant care.

17

MEDICARE PART B

Medicare Part B is the voluntary half of the Medicare program. Part B (also called the Supplementary Medical Insurance Plan) pays benefits to cover doctors' fees (including clinical psychologist, chiropractors, and podiatrists) and certain other services not covered under Part A. Part B will *not* cover routine physicals, vaccinations, hearing aids, and eye examinations (for glasses). Like Part A, Medicare Part B provides only limited benefits for those requiring long-term care.

Part B coverage is available to those eligible for Part A coverage. This type of coverage is automatic if you are receiving Social Security benefits unless you opt out of the program. Part B coverage is partially funded by the monthly premiums paid by the participants, although the vast majority of the funding is provided through taxation of wage earners and self-employed individuals. In 1991 the premium is $29.90. The premium amount is automatically deducted from your Social Security check.

Medicare Part B will pay, after the deductible is satisfied, 80 percent of approved charges. In 1991 the deductible is $100. The definition of "approved charge" is important to understand. Each year a survey is conducted on a local basis to determine what doctors are charging for the services they perform. All the charges are first reviewed to determine the amount charged most frequently for each procedure. This is called the "customary charge." Next, an analysis is performed to determine how much a patient would have to spend to pay three out of every four doctor's charges for each service. This is the "prevailing charge." The least of these two numbers and the doctor's actual bill becomes the approved charge. It is possible for your doctor to charge you more than the approved amount. In that case, you will be liable for both the 20 percent Medicare coinsurance amount and 100 percent of the amount of the bill in excess of the approved amount.

Medicare Part B does provide certain outpatient benefits, including home care provided by a doctor. Home services, like other outpatient services, must be part of the doctor's plan of treatment. The types of home services covered are essentially the same as those involved in Part A. The home health care coverage pays 100 percent of the approved cost as long as it is medically necessary.

As is true with Part A, Medicare Part B is an inadequate shield against the problems of financing long-term care. The expenses associated with long-term care are for less skilled care, such as assistance with bathing, eating, dressing and other common activities. These services, while expensive, can be performed by someone far less skilled than a doctor or nurse. Consequently, Medicare doesn't solve the problem.

18

MEDICAID

Medicaid pays almost one half of the long-term care expenses for elderly nursing home residents. The tragedy of this statistic is that Medicaid is a welfare program for poor people. Many, if not most, of these Medicaid recipients entered the nursing home as solid members of the middle class—people who worked hard all their lives.

The Medicaid program is a joint program between the federal government and each of the 50 state governments. The federal regulations lay out broad guidelines within which the states must administer their programs. The job of administering the program and dealing with the public is then turned over to the state welfare bureaucracy. With so many different sets of rules, it is possible only to review the most general provisions of Medicaid.

Medicare, as you have seen, provides very little help to pay long-term care bills. Medicaid, on the other hand, does provide benefits that will pay for long-term care expenses such as custodial care in a nursing home.

Medicaid payments can only be made to long-term care facilities that are approved by the Medicaid authorities. To be approved, the facility must meet various guidelines and requirements about the quality of the building, rooms, and other physical aspects, as well as the quality of the care provided. Non-Medicaid facilities are sometimes among the best long-term care providers in a given area. So, if Medicaid is a possibility for you, it pays to learn whether your top choices for long-term care accept Medicaid recipients.

The Medicare Catastrophic Coverage Act was initially hailed as a major step forward in dealing with the problem of long-term care on a national level. The law contained major revisions to both the Medicare and Medicaid laws. Congress repealed the Medicare portion of the law, including the hated surtax, in 1989. However, the Medicaid changes were left untouched and remain in effect today.

To receive Medicaid benefits you must be "poor." There are various groups who either must be covered under federal law or who may be included at a state's discretion.

Medicaid also may provide benefits to senior citizens who are "medically needy." You are medically needy, generally speaking, if your income, after deducting for certain allowable expenses and your medical expenses, is less than an allowable standard. Asset limitations are also imposed. With Medicaid, if your assets (called "countable resources" in Medicaid jargon) exceed allowable limits, you will be required to "spend down" until you are sufficiently poor to be eligible for benefits. A few states (one of which is Florida) set strict income levels as well. If your income exceeds a certain level, Medicaid will be denied even if you have no assets.

One of the major changes brought by the Medicare Catastrophic Care Act that is still in effect is the so-called "spousal impoverishment rule." This rule, which took effect on October 1, 1989, requires that the income and assets of the "at-home spouse" must be taken into account when determining the eligibility of the spouse applying for Medicaid. The spouse is the only relative whose income and assets are deemed to be available to the person requiring long-term care. In "Medicaid-speak" the at-home spouse is called the "community spouse" and the spouse applying for Medicaid is called the "institutionalized spouse."

For purposes of determining Medicaid eligibilty, both spouses' assets are totalled and then divided equally between them. The community spouse is allowed to keep his or her own income (e.g., pension, Social Security, and interest on solely owned certificates of deposit) and one half of joint income. The community spouse may also be eligible for certain income allowances from the institutionalized spouses share. The community spouse may receive an allowance out of the institutionalized spouse's share of the income if the community spouse's share of joint income plus solely owned income is less than the federal poverty line for a family of two. This allowance is called the Monthly Maintenance Needs allowance.

Another possible allowance is the Family Dependent Allowance. This applies if a dependent parent, brother, sister, or child of the institutionalized spouse lives with the community spouse. The allowance is equal to one third of the amount by which a certain percentage of the federal poverty line for a family of two exceeds the dependent's income.

The other permitted allowance is called the Excess Shelter Allowance. This allowance is designed to alleviate the problem of a community spouse having unmanageable housing expenses. The amount of the allowance equals the amount by which the community spouse's expenses for rent, mortgage payments, insurance, utilities, and property taxes exceeds 30 percent of 122 percent of the federal poverty line for a family of two.

The total of the community spouse's share of income plus the Family Dependent Allowance and the Excess Shelter Allowance may not exceed $1,500 as adjusted for inflation. Appeal procedures are available through the courts and Medicaid system if you believe the amount allowed for the community spouse is too low.

Assets (or "countable resources") must also be combined. The community spouse is permitted to retain assets worth at least (in 1991) $13,296 and up to $66,480, depending on the state involved. Some larger states, such as New York, Florida, and California, have adopted the $66,480 allowance. Certain assets are exempt from consideration. These exempt items generally include the homestead (provided certain conditions are met), a car, a small burial fund, and personal effects. In the process of allocating assets, a "snapshot" of the items owned and their value is taken as of the date of institutionalization. The community spouse has appeal rights, either through the courts or the Medicaid system, if he or she believes that the resource allowance is so low it will cause a hardship.

The Medicaid recipient is generally allowed to keep nonexempt resources of about $2,000 to $2,500, depending on the state and circumstances involved. The Medicaid recipient is allowed to keep a $30 personal allowance out of his or her income to pay unreimbursed medical expenses. Finally, under certain circumstances, a single Medicaid recipient may be able to keep a home maintenance allowance if the doctor believes the recipient will be able to return home within six months.

The state does have some rights to recover the Medicaid benefits it has paid on behalf of the elderly nursing home resident. In some cases, a lien may be placed on the Medicaid recipient's home and other real property. Recovery on the lien is only permitted after the death of the recipient and surviving spouse. Recovery may be further limited if certain relatives still live in the home. In some cases, recovery of benefits can also be made from the recipient's estate.

19

QUALIFYING FOR MEDICAID

Medicaid is generally viewed as the solution of last resort. Like other welfare programs, Medicaid is a safety net. However, for some people who have not undertaken other planning steps, Medicaid may be the only option. What strategies can you use to qualify for Medicaid without first surrendering virtually all of your assets to the nursing home or other care provider?

Medicaid-qualifying strategies have strong appeal. Senior citizens have worked long and hard to accumulate their life's savings. It seems particularly unfair that they should have to spend most, if not all, of their savings before they can obtain the help they need. The loss of their savings will not only permanently alter their own life-style but will effectively disinherit their children and other loved ones from whatever legacy might have otherwise been available.

When deciding to qualify for Medicaid without "spending down" to poverty levels, people sometimes are torn by a difficult emotional conflict. On the one hand, there is a certain pride that most people have in being able to take care of themselves and provide for their own needs. They are proud of the fact that, in spite of wars, depressions, and other hard times, they have never needed a "handout"; they've never been "on the dole." They may have even looked down on welfare recipients and wondered why "those people" didn't just find a job. The notion of intentionally becoming one of "those people" on welfare is abhorrent to many.

On the other hand, those faced with the need to consider Medicaid have probably been significant taxpayers over the years. The program is there and they helped pay for it, so why not take advantage of the system now that they need it? Most people do not feel guilty about arranging their affairs to take advantage of, say, an income tax deduction, even if it means that someone else may have to pay higher taxes. Some would argue that Medicaid is no different. After all, some of the Medicaid rules appear to have contemplated people taking steps to qualify for Medicaid while preserving at least some wealth for their heirs.

The obvious strategy to qualify for Medicaid is to transfer assets from the person about to apply for Medicaid to some third person, such as a family member. Remember, transferring assets between spouses generally, does not remove the assets from consideration for Medicaid eligibility. It would seem simple just to give away your assets to a son or daughter, thus impoverishing yourself, and then apply for Medicaid. In fact, that is too simple. Congress has foreseen this strategy and provided rules that govern the transfer of assets for less than full value before applying for Medicaid. The new rules are part of the Medicare Catastrophic Care Act and apply to transfers made after June 30, 1988.

Under the new rules, states are required to deny a person eligibility for Medicaid if they have made transfers for less than fair value within 30 months of applying for Medicaid. The period of ineligibility lasts for the shorter of (1) 30 months or (2) a period of time equal to the value of the assets given away divided by the average local monthly cost for a nursing home resident. For example, Vivian suffers from Alzheimer's disease and will soon enter a nursing home. She and her husband, Jack, transferred a $20,000 municipal bond from

61

her name to their son's name. Vivian then applied for Medicaid. The average local monthly cost for a nursing home is $2,000. Therefore, Vivian will be ineligible for Medicaid for ten months ($20,000 bond/$2,000 per month).

There are certain exempted transfers. Special rules apply to gifts of the family home. The ineligibility rule does not apply to transfers of the home to the community spouse or to a blind or disabled child. You may also transfer your home to a dependent child or your brother or your sister, provided they had an equity interest in the home for at least a year. Transfers of the home to children who have helped care for the Medicaid applicant while living in the home for two years are also excepted.

Transfers of any other asset to the community spouse are exempt as are transfers of any asset to a blind or disabled child. However, these assets may not be re-transferred later to another third party by the community spouse or the blind/disabled child. A transfer may also be exempt if you can prove that the transfer was made for reasons other than to qualify for Medicaid or that a denial of benefits will work an undue hardship. Finally, transfers of assets in exchange for other valuable assets are permitted.

Making gifts of assets to children or other loved ones can allow you to qualify for Medicaid. Two caveats are in order. First, be sure to leave sufficient assets in your own name to cover up to 30 months of nursing home or other expenses until you become eligible for Medicaid. Second, you should be aware that large gifts (over $10,000) to any one individual can trigger federal gift tax consequences. The federal gift tax is discussed in Key 43.

Another strategy is to convert a nonexempt asset into an exempt asset. For instance, cash in a savings account or certificate of deposit may be used to pay off a home mortgage or to make a substantial improvement to your home. Of course, converting a liquid asset, such as a savings account, may have negative repercussions if the Medicaid applicant dies soon after the home improvement is made and the surviving spouse or other heir needs access to cash.

A "Medicaid Qualifying Trust" may also be used. A Medicaid Qualifying Trust is a trust (See Key 27 for further information on trusts) established by the Medicaid applicant for his or her own benefit or by the applicant's spouse. Under the Medicaid rules, the applicant is deemed to have the maximum amount the trustee could distribute to the applicant, whether or not the trustee actually distributes that amount. To the extent that the applicant has access to the income or principal of the trust, the transfer may not trigger the 30-month disqualification rule. However, if someone other than the community spouse is made a beneficiary, the 30-month rule may be triggered. Gift tax considerations also come into play.

A trust can also be set up by a third person for the benefit of the Medicaid applicant. To avoid having the applicant's interest as a beneficiary of the trust counted as income or a resource for Medicaid, these trusts are usually designed as "luxury trusts" or "discretionary trusts." Sometimes the third party has acquired the assets placed in the trust from the applicant and then placed those same assets into the luxury or discretionary trust. The initial transfer to the third party may trigger the 30-month disqualification rule and may involve gift tax implications. The second transfer may also involve gift tax consequences. These trusts must be drafted very carefully to avoid running afoul of the Medicaid rules. The guidance of an experienced attorney is essential.

20

PRIVATE HEALTH INSURANCE

If Medicare won't pay most long-term custodial care expenses and if Medicaid is only the last resort, will private health insurance pick up the tab? Probably not. Senior citizens are a prime target market for a variety of health insurance products. Most of these effectively address insuring real health risks. Unfortunately, some are of dubious value. This chapter addresses the major forms of health insurance available to senior citizens. Keys 21 through 24 specifically address nursing home or long-term care insurance.

Five different types of health insurance policies are available to senior citizens to augment the coverage provided by Medicare:

- Medicare supplement policies
- Health Maintenance Organizations
- Major medical policies
- Hospitalization indemnity policies
- Dread disease policies

Medicare supplement policies are owned by about 70 percent of all Medicare recipients. They are also sometimes called Medigap policies because, in theory, they fill in the gaps in Medicare coverage. Medicare supplement policies are becoming more standard. Congress has given a group of state insurance regulators (the National Association of Insurance Commissioners) the ability to create a system of uniform minimum standards for Medicare supplement policies.

The new standards seek to simplify these policies. The current mishmash of different policies will be replaced by ten standard policies. Each of the ten policies will offer a different package of features and benefits. All of the new policies must provide certain coverages with additional benefits available on more comprehensive policies.

Generally, Medicare supplement policies cover only the types of services covered by Medicare. Medicare provides only limited benefits for skilled nursing care and some home care. Even under the new Medicare supplement regulations, the insurance company is not required to provide benefits to cover the gaps in these limited areas. Because Medicare does not provide adequate protection against long-term care needs, generally neither will a Medicare supplement policy.

A Health Maintenance Organization (HMO) is really a system of prepaying for medical services rather than an insurance policy in the strict sense. Members of HMOs pay a fee (often monthly) for their membership, allowing them access to the physicians and other health care professionals employed by the HMO. The HMO will often provide broader coverage than a Medicare supplement policy, sometimes at a lower cost. One disadvantage of HMOs is that your choice of doctors is limited to those who participate in the HMO plan. Another disadvantage is that an HMO generally does not provide any long-term custodial care benefits.

Major medical policies are designed to help pay for the hospital and doctor bills resulting from a serious illness or injury. These policies usually do not pay benefits until medical costs are quite high and generally do little to offset the out-of-pocket cost of Medicare deductible provisions. These policies may be purchased individually, through groups, or through a current or former employer. They are not ordinarily designed to cope with the costs of long-term custodial care.

The other two forms of health insurance—hospitalization and dread disease—generally provide a fixed daily benefit for each day of a covered event. A hospitalization indemnity policy will pay a fixed dollar amount for each day you are confined to a hospital, within policy limits. A dread disease policy will pay a fixed benefit for each specified type of treatment received for a particular disease (for example, cancer). Both of these types of policies may provide cash that can be used to offset medical expenses not covered by Medicare or other insurance. However, the offset will occur more by coincidence than design. The gaps in Medicare coverage can be filled more efficiently using the other types of policies.

Filling the gaps in Medicare coverage is a critical issue for most senior citizens. Those at or near the Medicaid income and asset limits may not need additional coverage if Medicaid is likely to be available. For seniors with modest means (but above Medicaid eligibility), an HMO may be the most cost-effective alternative. Do not make the common mistake of buying more than one Medicare supplement policy with overlapping coverage. The new federal law is designed to help prevent people from buying overlapping coverage. However, senior citizens who want to shift the risk of long-term care to an insurance company should look to the long-term care or nursing home policies specifically designed for that risk.

21

LONG-TERM CARE INSURANCE—AN OVERVIEW

Long-term care insurance is a relatively new type of insurance. Some insurance companies have been offering insurance that covers skilled nursing home care for a number of years. Policies designed to deal specifically with long-term *custodial* care are far more recent.

The number of insurance companies offering long-term care insurance has mushroomed in recent years. As recently as 1983, only 16 companies were writing long-term care insurance. Today, more than 100 companies provide this coverage. The number of policies has also exploded, from about 70,000 in 1985 to well over one million today. Long-term care coverage is expected to be a rapidly expanding line of business for insurance companies. Some estimate that by the year 2000 as many as 30 percent of all working and retired adults will be covered.

The most common type of long-term care policy pays a fixed dollar benefit for each day you are in a nursing home. Some offer home care coverage as well. A few policies cover only home care. Most of these policies are individually owned by the insured. Group coverage is just starting and probably will become more common.

Another relatively recent innovation is so-called "living benefits" life insurance policies. These policies are standard cash value life insurance contracts with a special provision allowing at least a portion of the "death" benefit to be paid when you enter a nursing home, become terminally ill, or encounter some other specified event. Living benefits life policies are covered in Key 25. Keys 23 and 24 concentrate on individually owned, traditional long-term care policies.

Keep in mind that purchasing a long-term care policy is only one strategy in long-term care planning and should be done only if shifting the financial risk of long-term care to an insurance company is appropriate in your situation. Applying the financial planning process and working with a team of advisors will help you assess whether buying such a policy is a good idea. As a rough guide, if you have assets (other than your house and personal belongings) of $1 million or more, you may not need long-term care insurance. You probably have sufficient assets to pay for most reasonably foreseeable long-term care possibilities. If your assets are less than $100,000, you may not have sufficient resources to pay for the premiums of a high-quality policy. In the case of long-term care insurance, a poor policy often is the same or worse than no policy at all.

To purchase a long-term care policy, a four-step approach is suggested. First, purchase the policy only from a reputable and knowledgeable individual. Key 6 will provide you with some guidance in this area. Second, only purchase a policy underwritten by a financially strong insurance company. Key 22 deals with this issue. Third, learn the basic provisions available in long-term care policies. These are explained in Key 23. Finally, evaluate several policies to select the one best suited to your needs. Key 24 explains evaluating long-term care policies and Appendix A provides a checklist to use when comparing policies.

22

SELECTING AN INSURER

The first step in selecting an insurance policy is to select a good insurance company. After all, the greatest policy in the world will do precious little if the insurance company is unable to meet its obligations. Three areas should be reviewed: financial strength, customer service, and underwriting philosophy.

Evaluating the financial strength of a large insurance company is an impossible task for the average person. It is also impossible for the average accountant, attorney, and insurance agent. Fortunately, you don't have to be a financial analyst knowledgeable in the arcane rules of insurance statutory accounting principals to evaluate the financial strength of any insurance company because four widely recognized independent rating agencies have already done the work for you. All you have to understand is their rating system.

The oldest and by far the largest rating service (in terms of number of companies rated) is the A. M. Best Company. A. M. Best publishes *Best's Insurance Reports—Life-Health,* which provides the most comprehensive ratings of the more than 100 companies that currently offer long-term care coverage in one form or another. Best's ratings are designed to give you information about how well the insurance company has performed relative to its peers and its ability to live up to policy obligations. Its ratings go from A+ (Superior) to C− (Fair).

Three other companies—Moody's Investor Service, Duff and Phelps, and Standard & Poor's—also rate the financial strength of insurance companies. Moody's ranks firms from Aaa for exceptional firms to C for the lowest quality firms. Under Moody's system, insurers with ratings of Baa to Aaa are considered strong, and those rated Ba to C are considered weak. Duff and Phelps uses a scale that ranges from AAA for those companies with the best ability to pay claims to CCC– for firms that have been, or are likely to be, placed under the supervision of one or more state insurance commissions. Using the Duff and Phelps ratings, companies that are rated AA– to AAA have at least a very high ability to pay claims. Standard & Poor's also uses a letter rating system, but its system ranges from AAA to D. Firms rated AAA to BB are considered to have a "secure" ability to pay claims. Firms rated AAA have a "superior" claims paying ability, and BB rated firms are judged to have only an "average" claims paying ability. Insurers rated B to D are considered to have claims paying ability that is "speculative." Firms rated D are under liquidation supervised by one or more state insurance commissioners.

Insurance company actuaries rely on historical information to make their predictions of future claims. These predictions are used to determine the premiums you pay. If the insurance company estimates too low, the premiums may not be enough to pay future claims and the insurance company will have to make up the difference out of its reserves. Because long-term care policies do not have the long historical track records associated with other types of insurance, there is a greater chance that the actuaries' claims estimates may be low. Therefore, it is very important when purchasing a long-term care policy to purchase the policy from a strong insurer.

Virtually every major insurance company has been rated by A. M. Best. Many, however, have no rating from the other three services. The lack of a rating from one or more of the other three services is not necessarily a bad sign. The other three services are relatively new at rating insurers and they simply don't cover as many companies. You should look for a long-term care insurer that has an A or A+ rating from A. M. Best. Don't purchase a policy from a lower rated company. If the company is rated by one of the other three agencies, check the rating to make sure it is consistent with the A. M. Best rating. If the ratings are inconsistent (for example, an A from Best's and a Ba from Moody's) investigate further.

The long-term care insurance agent should be able to tell you the ratings for any company he or she represents. Insist that the agent provide you with written documentation of the company's rating from all the services that provide a rating. In addition, you can investigate the ratings on various companies in many local libraries. The rating services publications are generally found in the business reference or the general reference section.

The insurer's reputation for customer service is also important. If you have a question about a claim, you want an insurer that will respond fairly and promptly. You can check on the company, and in many cases the agent, by contacting the insurance commissioner in your state. The insurance commissioner's office will generally have an office of consumer affairs or similar division to handle your inquiry. You may also consult your local Better Business Bureau.

Underwriting philosophy is something that most consumers fail to consider. Underwriting is the process insurance companies go through to determine whether they want to accept you as a risk. Insurance companies want to insure the people who are least likely to make a claim. You want to select an insurer that pays fairly when there is a claim, but is not forced to pay an inordinately large number of claims. After all, insurers that pay too many claims sometimes go out of business.

Two principle underwriting philosophies are popular in long-term care policies. Some companies do most of their underwriting when a claim is made. Some have called this practice a "back end" philosophy. Companies that use a back end philosophy tend to ask few health-related questions during the application process. The policies are deceptively easy to obtain. If you have a claim, however, the insurance company then thoroughly reviews the claim and your medical history to determine if there is a reason to deny the claim on the terms of the policy. Other companies do their underwriting at the time the application is made. These policies have applications that ask a larger number of detailed questions about your health. You are more likely to be turned down by a company that does its underwriting "up front." You are also far more likely to have a hassle-free claim, assuming you answered all the questions on the application truthfully. Deal only with companies that use up front underwriting.

23

LONG-TERM CARE POLICY FEATURES

Long-term care insurance has received a great deal of attention in the popular press. The quality of long-term care policies has improved dramatically in recent years; however, it still pays to compare policies very carefully. A large number of policies written today do not incorporate many of the latest features.

To compare long-term care policies, you must understand some of the standard provisions contained in those policies. This Key reviews some of the important provisions of long-term care policies. The next Key focuses on those features that should be in your policy and those features you should avoid.

Type of Contract. Long-term care policies are usually considerd indemnity type contracts. They pay you a fixed benefit generally per day, for every day you are entitled to benefits under the policy. Sometimes the daily benefit exceeds your actual nursing home or home health care cost. Some policies pay the full benefit, regardless of your actual cost. Another type of policy pays the lower of the daily benefit or your actual cost.

Daily Benefit. The typical long-term care policy will give you a range of daily benefits from which to choose. For example, the policy might pay a benefit of from $30 to $100 per day, in $10 increments. The ability to select a daily benefit allows you to tailor your policy to the costs of nursing homes in your area. Obviously, the greater the daily benefit, the more expensive the policy.

Guaranteed Renewable. If your policy is guaranteed renewable, your insurance company cannot cancel your policy for any reason, other than nonpayment of premium. This feature allows you to retain coverage even if your health deteriorates. The insurance company also cannot raise your premium unless it raises the premium for everyone in your state with a similar policy.

Eligibility. Eligibility determines the ages that the insurance company is willing to cover. The low end of the age range is usually around 45. Insurance companies typically will not insure you if you are over 85. Many will put substantial restrictions on the features if you are over 75 or 80. Age plays a very large role in the cost of the insurance. The younger you are, the lower your insurance premium.

Level of Care. As we have seen, there are three levels of nursing home care—skilled, intermediate, and custodial. A long-term care policy defines the level of care covered by the policy.

Prior Hospitalization. Some long-term care policies, like Medicare, require prior hospitalization for a specified period of time to qualify for benefits. However, a substantial number of nursing home patients, particularly those with degenerative conditions such as Alzheimer's disease, go directly from their home to the nursing home. The prior hospitalization features is one of the major sources of criticism of long-term care policies. Policies issued by companies in the forefront of this area do *not* have a prior hospitalization requirement. Some policies also require some prior higher level of nursing home care before they will pay for custodial care.

Organic Brain Disorders. The typical long-term care policy does not cover nursing home stays for mental illness. The policy, however, should contain clear language that organic brain disorders, such as Alzheimer's disease and other forms of senile dementia, are covered.

Preexisting Conditions. Preexisting conditions are a critically important feature of any policy. This term determines what, if any, benefits will be payable if your nursing home stay was caused by a medical condition that predated your application for the policy. Some policies contain no restrictions on benefits for preexisting conditions. Other policies do not provide coverage if the nursing home stay occurs within a specified period (for example, six months) of the issuance of the policy and if the stay is the result of a preexisting condition. Finally, some policies may never pay benefits if you require nursing home care due to a preexisting condition.

Elimination Period. The elimination period determines how many days of nursing home care you must receive before benefits are payable. Some policies allow you to select an elimination period of zero days; benefits are paid from the first day of nursing home confinement. Or, you may extend the elimination period up to 100 days or more of nursing home care before a benefit is paid. You can reduce the cost of a long-term care policy by increasing the elimination period.

Inflation Protection. The cost of nursing home care, like other medical expenses, is rising faster than the general rate of inflation. A daily benefit of $60 per day may seem adequate given your circumstances today. If nursing home costs rise seven percent a year, however, that cost will be $120 in about ten years. You may pay long-term care premiums for twenty years or more, so it pays to consider inflation. Insurers appear to have settled on two ways to account for inflation. Some policies allow you to purchase a benefit that is adjusted each year (usually the lesser of some fixed percentage or inflation). Other policies give you the option of purchasing additional coverage periodically. These latter policies provide guaranteed insurability for these additional purchases.

Benefit Period. The benefit period defines how long benefits will be paid. Benefits may be payable for a set period of time, for example, two to four years. Other policies have both a per stay and a lifetime cap—for example, two years per stay in a nursing home up and to five years over your life. Still others may allow you to choose benefits that are payable for life.

Home Care. In addition to covering nursing home care, some policies also include coverage for home care services. Home health care coverage should be examined carefully. The quality of the coverage varies extensively. The amount of the daily benefit may differ from the nursing home benefit. The benefit period may also differ. A prior nursing home stay may be required.

Triggering Event. Some event must trigger the payment of benefits. Insurance companies want to protect themselves from paying claims for nursing home stays that are undertaken for mere convenience. They have come up with two different triggers. Under one type of trigger, the policy pays benefits if a doctor certifies that your nursing home confinement (or need for home health care) is "medically necessary." A growing trend among some insurance carriers is to base the payments on your inability to perform certain "activities of daily life" (ADLs). Some policies go further and consider a mental, rather than physical, inability to perform an ADL. For example, a patient with Alzheimer's disease may have the dexterity to dress himself or herself but may not understand *why* getting dressed is necessary.

Waiver of Premium. Some policies allow the policy premium to be waived while you receive benefits.

24

EVALUATING LONG-TERM CARE POLICIES

Buying a long-term care policy is, in many respects, similar to buying many other products. Over the years you have probably learned these three rules of shopping: First, the more you know about a product, the better your chances of getting a good deal. Second, you get what you pay for. Finally, if something sounds too good to be true, it probably is. Keeping these simple rules in mind will help you make an informed decision about a long-term care insurance policy.

Long-term care insurance is one of the newest and fastest changing areas of insurance coverage. No uniform regulations require policies to meet nationwide minimum standards, although some regulatory bodies and consumer groups are moving in that direction. New carriers enter the business regularly. Some carriers have already abandoned the business, unable to make a profit. Policies change frequently. The increased competition generally has worked in favor of the consumer as insurance companies offer improvements to their policies to keep up with the competition. Nevertheless, be very cautious and careful when evaluating long-term care policies because premium costs and policy benefits vary widely.

When evaluating policies, be sure to evaluate more than one policy. It is often convenient to work with an insurance agent who represents more than one company. If your agent represents only one company, you will need to deal with at least one more agent.

A long-term care insurance policy should cover the

major risks associated with long-term care, have terms that allow the payment of the amount of coverage you need when you need it, and be cost effective.

Your long-term care policy should cover the major risks of long-term care. The policy must cover all three levels of nursing home care—skilled, intermediate, and custodial—and it must cover those risks without requiring *any* prior hospitalization or prior higher level nursing home services. The policy must also cover organic brain disorders, such as Alzheimer's disease. The coverage should be available upon the doctor's diagnosis of an indication of Alzheimer's or other disorder because a final and definite diagnosis of these illnesses is not currently possible except through an autopsy. Most policies will deny coverage for preexisting conditions for some period of time after the policy is issued. Although a policy with no denial of coverage for preexisting conditions is preferable, do not buy a policy with an exclusion period of more than 6 months.

Most senior citizens would prefer to receive custodial care services at home. Coverage for home care services is a highly desirable feature, even though it will add to the cost of the policy. The benefit should be payable without prior nursing home (any level) or hospital confinement. Because home care is generally less costly for you than nursing home care, if you find that the addition of home care coverage makes a policy unaffordable, you will probably be better off with a good policy that covers only nursing homes than with no policy at all.

The amount and time of payment of the benefit are the other critical components of the policy. The amount of the basic benefit can be tied to the cost of nursing home services in your area. If you are considering a move, perhaps to live closer to family or to a sunnier climate, check into the cost of nursing homes in that area as well. The amount of your daily benefit could be set equal to the cost of a nursing home in your area if you want to shift as much of the risk as possible to the insurance company. If you are willing to shoulder part of the burden of paying the nursing home, a lower amount of daily benefit may be selected. In any case, with the national average cost for nursing homes between $60 and $80 per day, a daily benefit in that range seems an appropriate target. It is also preferable, but not necessarily critical, to find a policy that pays the daily benefit even if your actual cost is less.

Because the cost of care continues to go up, your coverage should also go up. Consider only policies that provide inflation protection. Insurance companies charge an additional premium for the inflation rider, but it's usually worth the cost. Policies that build an inflation rate formula into the contracts are preferable to those that guarantee your insurability. With the formula inflation rates, you pay the additional coverage with each payment, and you won't be surprised by big jumps in the premium associated with adding benefits later.

The period of time over which benefits are paid is also important. The *elimination period* will determine when benefits start, which could be as soon as the first day you enter the nursing home or as long as 100 or more days later. When choosing an elimination period, remember that insurance works best to cover true economic disasters, not minor problems, which are much more likely to occur. Therefore, the cost to insure against a small loss is relatively much more expensive than the insurance against a major loss. Set the elimination period as long as possible given your ability to pay nursing home bills. The longer the elimination period, the lower your premium. The premium you save can be put back in your pocket, or, preferably, used to extend the period during which benefits are paid.

The benefit period will determine the length of time you receive the daily benefit after the elimination period. The longer the benefit period, the better. A lifetime benefit is preferred, but it is also the most expensive. Further, some companies will not write a lifetime contract if you are beyond a specified age (for example, 75 or 80) when you first apply. Keep in mind that Medicaid, your last resort, has a waiting period of 30 months after gratuitous transfers before benefits are payable. Also remember that roughly half of all nursing home stays last between 30 and 40 months. Therefore, a benefit payable for at least three years seems an appropriate minimum.

The premium charged by the insurance company should be fixed. Avoid policies that increase your premium as you get older. The policy should also be "guaranteed renewable," that is, the insurance company cannot cancel your policy except for nonpayment of premiums (See Key 23).

Long-term insurance can be expensive. But, so is the risk of long-term care. The better policies may also be the most expensive. Be warned, though, that a "cheap" policy may be worse than no policy at all. Contracts that contain restrictive provisions may *never* pay claims.

How much will you have to spend? Cost depends on many factors. First, cost varies according to your age at the time you buy the policy. The younger you are, the less expensive the coverage. Some have estimated that the same policy purchased at age 65 may cost double or even almost triple for a 75-year-old. Most people don't need long-term care until they are well into their 70s and 80s. By then, however, they may not be able to obtain any insurance or the insurance that they can obtain is unaffordable. Many people start to think about the possibility of long-term care when they consider their own retirement, probably when they are in their

50s and early 60s. This is an excellent time to lock in the favorable rates offered to younger people buying long-term care policies.

The amount of the policy is also affected by a number of other factors:

- The higher the daily benefit, the shorter the elimination period. The longer the benefit period, the higher the premium.
- Your health also affects the premium. Healthy people will get more favorable rates than those who have significant health risks.
- In general, any factor or term of the policy that tends to increase the chance that the insurance company will pay a claim or that the claim will be larger, will tend to increase the premium.

Determining what is a "reasonable premium" for a long-term care policy is extremely difficult. The policies change very rapidly and the cost of the policy depends on numerous variables. One fairly recent study of nine roughly comparable policies found annual premiums of over $1,200 at age 65, about $1,800 at age 70, almost $2,900 at age 75, and just under $3,900 at age 79. Use these figure as "ballpark" numbers only.

25

GE option?
S+SP ma only

LIVING BENEFITS LIFE INSURANCE

Traditionally, life insurance has fulfilled two roles. First, it provided cash to make up for the loss of earnings resulting from the untimely death of a family bread-winner. Second, it provided cash to pay debts, funeral expenses, estate taxes, probate expenses, and other cash or so-called "liquidity" needs arising because of someone's death. Traditional whole life insurance has always provided some benefits during the insured's life through the policy's cash value, which could either be borrowed out of the policy or received upon surrender. Very recently a number of life insurance companies have added a "living benefits" feature to their life insurance policies, which may have some application to providing funds to meet long-term care expenses.

Living benefits life insurance policies grew out of the problems terminally ill patients sometimes faced in meeting financial obligations. These individuals often felt a need to resolve their financial obligations while they were alive, and some insurance companies responded, at first voluntarily, by advancing a portion of the death benefit. Today, about 70 insurance companies offer some form of living benefits life insurance, and over 40 states permit its use.

A living benefits life insurance policy allows the owner of the policy to access some portion of the "death" benefit or face amount of the policy during life. The benefit is not a loan or policy surrender. Rather, some portion of the death benefit is paid if certain conditions are met. The amount that is accessible depends

82

on the terms of the policy. The amount of the death benefit you will be able to receive may range from about 25 percent of the death benefit to virtually the entire death benefit. Generally, what is paid out in the form of living benefits comes at the expense of the beneficiaries of the death benefit. The living benefits may be paid in a lump sum or monthly, depending on the policy and the nature of your claim.

There are generally three types of living benefits life insurance, all of which are a variation on cash value life policies. The first type pays a benefit in the event you are diagnosed as terminally ill. Your doctor may have to certify that you have been diagnosed as having only, for example, two years or less to live. The size of the benefit you will be able to receive depends on the terms of the policy. The payment of the benefit may or may not wipe out any benefit your heirs might otherwise receive.

Another type of living benefits feature pays a benefit if you are diagnosed as having some serious illness such as cancer. The illness does not necessarily have to be terminal. The amount of the benefit you may receive under this type of policy is usually a smaller percentage of the death benefit than is generally available under a terminal illness type policy.

The third type of living benefits policy pays a benefit, usually monthly, in the event you are confined to a nursing home. The type of facility may be restricted to a skilled nursing home whereas other, better policies, will cover all three levels of care. The amount of the benefit is equal to some percentage, usually two percent, of the death benefit up to some specified limit. For example, assume you own a $50,000 life insurance policy that permits you to receive two percent of the death benefit every month you are in a custodial care nursing home, up to 50 percent of the death benefit.

Under this policy, when you enter the nursing home you will begin receiving $1,000 per month until you have received a total of $25,000 over 25 months.

The living benefits feature is sometimes made available as a no-cost or low-cost rider or amendment to an existing life insurance policy. In general, the greater the potential benefit, the more expensive the rider. A living benefits feature may also be part of a new life insurance policy. This addition will generally increase the premium cost for the policy, sometimes significantly.

The great appeal to using living benefits life occurs if it can be added to an existing policy at little or no cost. However, these policies do involve some important considerations. First, for long-term care, you must find a policy or rider that covers custodial care. The terminal illness or dread disease policies are of little use for long-term care. Next, you must examine the provisions of any policy that offers a nursing home feature. You should be sure that it will offer the same probability of paying benefits as a good, traditional long-term care policy (See Key 23). The cost of these policies can also be very high, particularly if you are trying to buy a new policy of life insurance later in life, and your health is not what it used to be.

There are also unresolved tax questions surrounding these policies. Benefits payable at death under a life insurance policy and benefits received under a health insurance policy, such as with a traditional long-term care insurance policy, are income-tax free. However, no one is certain whether the benefits payable during life under a living benefits policy will be income-tax free. The Internal Revenue Service (IRS) simply has not ruled on the issue. You should take this into consideration before purchasing such a policy.

Some would argue that living benefits life insurance policies are too great a compromise. Life insurance tends to work best when it is purchased to fulfill a life insurance need. Asking a good life insurance policy to also be a good long-term care policy may be asking too much. The designers of the policy may have to make compromises that result in a policy that is not good at accomplishing either task.

When selecting long-term care coverage you compare a living benefits policy to a traditional, health-insurance type long-term care policy. If you can benefit from a life insurance policy, and the living benefits are available at a fair price, a living benefits policy may be in order.

26

GUARDIANSHIPS

Individuals who are confined to long-term care facilities or who are receiving custodial care services at home are sometimes limited in their ability to make financial and health-related decisions and require the assistance of others. Nurses and doctors help keep you well; but they can't pay your bills, file your tax return, manage your investments, or even approve a particular course of treatment. The laws of each state provide a mechanism to make these decisions for those who are no longer able to make them. This chapter provides an overview of the procedures generally available under state law. Keys 27 through 31 provide an overview of some of the steps you can take to avoid the expense and complications of a court-supervised system.

The procedure to appoint someone to handle the financial and health affairs of another is usually called a "guardianship proceeding." A guardianship proceeding requires that someone, frequently a family member, must ask the court to declare another to be incompetent to handle financial matters and/or health decisions. The court involved may be the probate court for the county where the alleged incompetent resides.

To understand the guardianship process, it is necessary to understand some of the basic legal concepts. There are two basic parties to a guardianship: The "guardian" is the person appointed by the court to make decisions for another. The "ward" is the individual judged to be incapable of making any or all decisions. At one time or another we have all been guardians or wards. When we were children (people under 18 in most states) we were legal wards of our parents. Our mothers and fathers had the basic right to decide what medical treatment we would or would not receive. Our parents were also able to make whatever financial decisions were necessary because, as children, we were deemed incapable of making them on our own. You will sometimes see parents referred to as the "natural guardians" of their minor children.

Some states make a distinction between a guardian who is permitted to make financial decisions and a guardian who is able to make health-related decisions. It may be possible to have two guardians for one person, each with responsibility for a different type of decision. The guardian responsible for financial decisions is sometimes called the "guardian of the estate." Another term sometimes used for the financial decision maker is "conservator." The guardian responsible for health and other personal decisions is called the "guardian of the person." New York makes an interesting distinction. In that state, a "conservator" functions to assist someone who is disabled, but still competent, whereas the truly incompetent individual has a "committee" appointed by the court to be the substitute decision maker.

Having a guardian appointed is not a very complicated procedure. It begins when an "interested person" "petitions" the court to declare an individual incompetent and to appoint a guardian. The petition may ask the court to appoint a guardian for the person, a guardian for the estate, or both. The court may hear testimony from doctors, psychologists, social workers, family members, neighbors, or others to determine whether a person is incompetent. The person alleged to be incompetent may be present and may be represented by an attorney. The alleged incompetent may challenge the evidence supporting incompetence and present evidence supporting their competence. Frequently, however, guardianship proceedings are uncontested matters reluctantly brought by concerned family members.

The definition of incompetent varies from state to state, but generally some condition must be said to exist and some amount of reasoning ability must have been lost. The conditions typically include advancing age, medical conditions resulting from accident or illness, or addiction to drugs or alcohol. The loss of reasoning ability generally means that the person has lost the ability for self-care.

The court is generally bound by the statute of each state when determining who will be appointed as guardian. State law will typically give the judge a list, in descending order of preference, of the kinds of people who may be appointed guardian. Generally, courts prefer a family member over a court-appointed lawyer or other stranger, but depending on the circumstances, a stranger may be appointed.

The guardian may be required to file an "accounting" annually with the court. An accounting is a summary of all the incompetent person's items of income and expense. These accountings allow the court to review the nature of the expense items for the protection of the incompetent. In addition, the guardian may be required to post a "fidelity bond." A fidelity bond is a special type of insurance policy that pays a benefit to the incompetent person if the guardian misappropriates the assets placed in his or her care.

Once someone has been appointed as guardian, depending on the extent of the authority, he or she effectively becomes the legal substitute for the incompetent. If a doctor wants to perform surgery or other medical procedure, the guardian decides whether to proceed. If a bill needs to be paid, the guardian writes the check. If a dividend check, pension check, Social

Security check, or other income is received, the guardian signs the checks, deposits the money, and makes the investment decisions. If an asset needs to be purchased or sold, the guardian makes that decision, too.

Guardianship proceedings are not pleasant. It is difficult enough to decide that loved ones are no longer capable of caring for themselves. It is doubly difficult to have to prove incompetence in court in front of a roomful of strangers. The elderly relative may, in some jurisdictions, be required to appear in court, adding to the emotional burden for everyone. These proceedings may also be expensive. Like most other legal matters, they are not "do-it-yourself" projects. The cost of the legal fees may be a problem for some. If an annual accounting is required, the trips to the courthouse do not end after the guardian is appointed. Finally, there is the time factor to consider. Having the court appoint a guardian can be time consuming. This lapse of time may only make the life of the incompetent more difficult. On balance, there are sufficient negative aspects to the guardianship process to warrant taking positive steps to avoid it.

27

REVOCABLE LIVING TRUSTS

A *living trust* is a very powerful estate and financial planning tool. Among the benefits of a living trust is the ability to use it to cope with the possibility of your own potential incapacity.

Before exploring the uses of a living trust in planning for long-term custodial care, you should understand the basics of trusts in general. A *trust* is an agreement involving three parties, the grantor, the trustee, and the beneficiary. Under a trust, the grantor (who is sometimes called the settlor or trustor) asks the trustee to take legal possession of certain assets (the corpus or principal of the trust), manage those assets, and distribute the income earned by trust assets to the beneficiaries in the manner and at the time the grantor directs.

There are basically two types of trusts. A trust created under the terms of your will is usually called a *testamentary trust*. The other type of trust is called a *living trust*. In some areas living trusts are called *inter vivos* trusts. In addition to being either living or testamentary, a trust may also be either revocable or irrevocable. The terms of a revocable trust may be changed by the grantor as often and as extensively (up to and including totally eliminating the trust) as the grantor wishes. An irrevocable trust may also be created during the life of the grantor. The terms of an irrevocable trust, for all intents and purposes, cannot be altered. This chapter reviews the use of *revocable living trusts* in planning for long-term care.

A revocable living trust can be used in planning for long-term care to provide an alternative to having a guardian for the estate or conservator appointed for the grantor of the trust. As mentioned previously, all trusts require three parties—the grantor, the trustee, and the beneficiary. Many times those three roles are fulfilled by three different people. With a revocable living trust, however, the grantor of the trust often wears all three hats. The trust typically provides that all of the income of the trust and as much of the principal as is necessary will be paid by the grantor/trustee to the grantor/beneficiary. The trust should also provide that if the grantor/trustee/beneficiary becomes incompetent, then a *successor trustee* can step in to manage the trust (this is the key for long-term care planning purposes). The successor trustee is still bound by the language of the trust to use all of the income and principal of the trust for the benefit of the grantor/beneficiary. If properly arranged, a revocable living trust can provide for a fairly seamless transition in managing your financial affairs. You should note that the laws of some states do not permit the same person to act as grantor, trustee and beneficiary.

The choice of a successor trustee should be made carefully. It is important to find someone who has the time to do the job properly. He or she should also have a certain empathy for you, your situation, and the needs of your family. The successor trustee should also be competent to handle your financial affairs. Some trustees, particularly corporate trustees, charge substantial fees for their services. You must analyze the cost of the services of a successor trustee and compare that cost to the benefits the potential successor offers.

You have basically three choices when selecting a successor trustee: your spouse, another family member, or a close friend; a trusted advisor, such as your attorney or accountant; or a financial institution, such as a bank or a trust company.

Your loved ones are probably the people most concerned about your health and welfare, so they are a natural choice for many people. It is also generally unlikely that a spouse, family member, or friend will charge much, if anything, for the service they provide. Unfortunately, a family member or friend may not be your best choice in some cases.

If your financial affairs are particularly complex, there is no guarantee that a family member will have the expertise necessary to manage your trust. Moreover, should your loved one die or become incapacitated, the search for another successor may be complicated. Finally, as unpleasant as this may seem, there have been numerous cases of friends and family members betraying the trust you place in them by looting trust assets for their own purposes. To minimize this possibility, many advisors recommend that noncorporate trustees be required to obtain a fidelity bond.

A trusted advisor is sometimes appointed as the successor trustee. Lawyers, accountants, and other financial professionals may well have technical expertise and experience well beyond that possessed by any loved one. In addition, these individuals may be well known to your family, giving them comfort and confidence in handling your affairs. On the other hand, just because an attorney is skilled in, for example, tax matters does not make him or her an expert investor. In addition, advisors are just as mortal and fallible as your family members. You still face the possibility of the untimely death or incapacity of your successor trustee or the fraudulent handling of your affairs.

Your final option when selecting a successor trustee is to use a professional trustee, such as a bank trust department or a trust company. Corporate trustees generally have at their disposal the resources necessary to handle virtually any size trust, regardless of complexity. Corporate trustees also will be able to provide the services as long as the company is in business. The fraud risk is also greatly reduced due to the internal controls put in place by corporate trustees, the audits they must undergo, and the financial strength of the company. There are, of course, disadvantages to using a corporate trustee. One of the greatest disadvantages is the cost. Corporate trustee services can be quite expensive. Many people are also concerned that a corporate trustee will lack the sensitivity needed to handle family matters. The level and quality of service provided by corporate trustees also varies from institution to institution and even among the various branch offices of the same institution.

Consulting with a competent estate planning attorney will help you decide the successor trustee that will work best for you.

The final consideration in using a living trust is the issue of funding. The successor trustee can only control and manage those assets placed in the trust. Too often, individuals create living trust arrangements with only a nominal amount controlled by the trust. In the event of incapacity, the trustee's hands are tied because there are no funds to manage.

There are generally two ways to fund a living trust. The first is to change the ownership of your assets from your name to the trust. This should be done with the assistance of the lawyer who drafted the trust. It should also be done in conjunction with any estate planning strategies you have in place.

The other way to fund the living trust is to use a *durable power of attorney,* a concept discussed in detail in Key 29. In general, the durable power of attorney empowers someone to gather your assets together after you have become incapacitated and place them in the trust. This strategy allows you to continue to manage your affairs normally until such time as you becomed incapacitated. This type of living trust is sometimes called a *springing trust* because it springs into existence only when you need it.

It's necessary to make a quick mention of the tax consequences of using a living trust. For the most part, there aren't any. In fact, the lack of significant tax consequences is actually an advantage of using a living trust. For income tax purposes, revocable living trusts are, essentially, ignored. Further, although a revocable living trust can contain provisions to dispose of trust assets to your family at death, the trust will provide no inherent estate tax advantages or disadvantages. For more detailed information on this topic, read Barron's *Keys to Estate Planning and Trusts.*

28

JOINT OWNERSHIP

A common method to cope with managing financial affairs in the event of long-term care is joint ownership of property. Although appropriate for certain minor items, joint ownership is not as useful a tool as the revocable living trust (Key 27) or the durable power of attorney (Key 29). This chapter focuses on joint ownership, particularly as it applies to bank accounts.

Joint ownership is an often misused term. Actually four forms of ownership can be created between two people. True *joint ownership* is also called *joint ownership with the right of survivorship* or *joint tenancy*. The element of survivorship distinguishes joint ownership. If an asset is owned jointly by two people, the one that lives the longest will wind up with 100 percent of the asset. For example, Jack and Jill are joint owners of some real estate. Jack has died. Jack's heirs have no right to the real estate held jointly with Jill. Jill now owns all the rights to the real estate.

Tenancy in common is often confused with joint ownership. If two people are tenants in common, they each have the right to dispose of their share of the property in any way they choose either during life or at death. Had Jack and Jill been tenants in common, Jack's heirs would be entitled to one-half the real estate owned with Jill at Jack's death.

Two forms of co-ownership exist only between married couples. Community property applies in nine states—Arizona, California, Idaho, Louisiana, Nevada, New Mexico, Texas, Washington, and, in a somewhat modified form, Wisconsin. Basically, under community property principals, husbands and wives each own one half of all property acquired during marriage. *Tenancy by the entirety* is recognized in some of the noncommunity property states. Tenancy by the entirety is a form of co-ownership between husbands and wives that includes the right of survivorship.

Typically, joint tenancy is used to cope with long-term care when an elderly person adds a child, other relative, or trusted friend as a joint tenant to various types of property. The purpose of the joint tenancy is to give the new joint tenant the ability to handle the affairs of the elderly person in the event he or she is unable. Frequently, the new joint tenant is included on the elderly person's bank accounts.

Depending on state law, the terms of the bank's account agreement, and the selection you make, four types of accounts may be created. Some joint bank accounts only permit withdrawals if *both* joint tenants sign the check or withdrawal request form. Other joint bank accounts allow either joint tenant to withdraw only up to one-half the account balance. The third type of account allows *either* joint tenant to withdraw *all* of the funds in the account at any time. Finally, some states and banks allow *joint accounts for convenience only*. With these accounts, the noncontributing joint tenant merely acts as the agent or on behalf of the contributing joint tenant (the elderly person) when making withdrawals. The differences among these four types of joint accounts all relate to the rights to the balance of the account during the lives of the joint tenants. The surviving joint tenant will generally inherit 100 percent of the balance of the account at the death of the first to die.

In spite of the apparent simplicity of using joint accounts, they should be used sparingly, if at all, for several reasons. First, even though the joint account is established while the elderly person was competent, if the elderly person later becomes incompetent, a guardianship or other proceeding may still be required to make withdrawals to pay long-term care and other bills. Second, the creation of a joint tenancy can have unintended estate, gift, and income tax implications that should be explored. Third, there is a real possibility that the noncontributing joint tenant might misapply some or all of the funds in the account for his or her own use. This unpleasant possibility should be considered, even if you want to add a child or other close relative as the joint account holder. Finally, because the surviving joint tenant controls the account, the creation of a joint tenancy may upset an otherwise well-established estate plan. This final potential problem deserves further explanation.

Consider the case of Shirley, a widow, and her three daughters—Carla, Gail, and Sheila. Shirley was 70 years old and in good health, but felt that she needed some help in managing her finances. She had about $200,000 in various money market, savings, and certificate accounts at four different banks in town. Shirley named her eldest daughter, Carla, as a joint tenant. All three daughters were married and had growing families of their own. Carla was chosen because she lives just a few miles from Shirley and does not work outside the home. The other two daughters lived thousands of miles away and were able to get back home, at most, about once a year. Shirley's will left her estate to her three daughters equally.

This arrangement appeared to be working for about three years until Shirley had a stroke. After that, Carla spent many hours caring not only for her mother's finances, but also cleaning her house, tending to her yard, and providing her mother emotional support. Shirley's condition worsened over the next year and a half. Carla worked tirelessly doing everything she could until her mother's death.

When Shirley died, she still had about $100,000 in the joint bank accounts and, except for a few personal belongings, those accounts were all that she owned. Carla became the owner of the bank accounts. She consulted an attorney who told her that the money was hers, even though her mother's will called for an even split. Her sisters were insisting on their share of the $100,000. Carla's husband seemed to think it was unfair that the sisters should receive a share because Carla did most of the caring for her mother. Carla was torn. This problem could have been avoided through the use of a revocable living trust or a durable power of attorney. In this case, the overuse of joint property may have caused more problems than it solved.

29

DURABLE POWER OF ATTORNEY

A *durable power of attorney* is another tool that can be used in planning for long-term care. A durable power of attorney allows you to appoint someone to carry on your financial affairs.

To understand a durable power of attorney, it is necessary to first understand power of attorney in general. A power of attorney is used to give one person the right to act on another person's behalf. The person who grants the power of attorney is called the "principal." The individual who is given the power is called the "attorney-in-fact." There are two types of powers of attorney—special and general.

A special power of attorney gives the attorney-in-fact the right to act for the principal in connection with a specific transaction or for some other limited purpose.

A general power of attorney is much broader, granting the attorney-in-fact the ability to do for you almost anything you could do for yourself. Effectively, a general power of attorney creates a legal "clone." Because of the broad powers granted by a general power of attorney, this option should be used very carefully. Further, the attorney in fact must be someone in whom you have the utmost trust.

Traditionally, powers of attorney expire under three circumstances: when revoked by the principal, when the principal dies, and when the principal becomes incapacitated. A durable power of attorney is "durable" because it does *not* expire if the principal is incapacitated. It is this durability that makes it such a useful tool in planning for long-term care. For long-term care purposes, durable powers of attorney are usually also general powers of attorney granting the attorney-in-fact very broad powers.

The attorney-in-fact can act in your behalf only when he or she is in possession of a properly drafted and executed power of attorney. Further, unless the proper steps are taken, powers of attorney are generally effective immediately upon execution. It is probably unwise to execute a general, durable power of attorney and immediately give it to your attorney-in-fact. An alternative might be to give the power to a trusted advisor with instructions to deliver it to the attorney-in-fact in the event you become unable to manage your affairs.

A popular solution to this problem in many states is to use a *springing durable power of attorney*. A springing power is effective only if you are unable to manage your own affairs. The springing power will contain language stating the circumstances under which you will be deemed unable to make decisions, thus giving effect to the power. For example, the power might require a written statement signed by two doctors certifying that, given your current medical condition, you are unable to manage your finances. The power also might contain language requiring the physicians to use the standards of incompetence used in the guardianship statute in rendering an opinion. Many advisors recommend that one of the physicians certifying your competence should be your regular doctor. Beware: Not all states recognize the concept of the springing durable power of attorney. Contact your lawyer to see if this type of power of attorney applies in your state.

30

LIVING WILLS

Long-term care involves difficult decisions. Some of these decisions concern your health and the care you will receive. This Key and Key 31 deal with health-care decisions.

Normally, adults make their own health care decisions. Generally speaking, you may decide to refuse treatment, even if this decision will result in a more serious illness or your death. This power to decide your own fate is fairly well settled until you can no longer make decisions for yourself.

If you lose the ability to make your own health care decisions, someone will be asked to make them for you. Your substituted decision maker may be your guardian (See Key 26). However, courts have found it very difficult to allow any substituted decision maker to decide to discontinue treatment or to elect a course of treatment that may shorten your life. The courts generally have tried to ascertain whether there is enough evidence to establish that the decision to discontinue treatment is the one you would make for yourself if you were able. The most difficult cases are those where there is no clear-cut evidence of what the incapacitated person would do. The courts have tended to resolve any doubt in favor of prolonging life.

Proving that your medical condition is one that you would not tolerate may be a very difficult proposition. It is an emotional nightmare for your family as they must prove, in open court, that you would prefer death to your present condition. Without planning, these decisions can become the most unbearable of any decisions associated with long-term care.

One technique often used when planning for a substituted health care decision maker is the so-called "living will." Most states have a statute specifically authorizing the use of living wills. However, some states do not recognize the concept and you should check with an attorney experienced in living wills to determine their status in your home state. You may also check with the Society for the Right to Die (250 West 57th Street, New York, NY 10107; (212) 246-6973). Some states have approved forms for living wills that can reduce the legal fees associated with drafting them. You may want to have an attorney draft a custom-designed living will to suit your particular situation.

A living will states the care you desire in the event that you are faced with a life-threatening condition. Some states will only recognize a living will executed after you have been diagnosed with a terminal illness. Others may require that the document be re-signed periodically to ensure that it is "fresh."

Even in the states that do not recognize the living will concept by statute, it may make sense to draft a living will. Your doctors and the courts will not be bound by the provisions of a nonstatutory living will. However, the essence of the cases involving substituted health care decision makers has been determining what the patient would decide if he or she were able. A nonstatutory living will may provide some guidance to the court allowing a substitute decision maker to make decisions in line with your wishes. For more information on wills, see Barron's *Keys To Preparing A Will.*

31

HEALTH CARE PROXY

Living wills, as discussed in Key 30, are useful tools to ensure that your wishes are followed if you are ever faced with a life-threatening illness or injury and are unable to make your own decisions about your care. But, what if you are no longer able to make your own decisions, and you are faced with a non-life threatening medical problem? In some states, a *health care proxy* or *durable power of attorney for health care* may be the answer. These two terms describe similar devices. This Key, for simplicity's sake, uses the term health care proxy.

A health care proxy is a specialized type of durable power of attorney. Powers of attorney were discussed in Key 29. In a health care proxy, a third party, for example, your spouse or child, is authorized to make health care decisions in the event you are unable to make them. In some states, you can delegate the authority to make life or death decisions. Other states may only permit substituted decision making if your condition is nonlife threatening. Several states have prescribed forms that must be used. In any case, legal drafting requirements must be met. Health care proxies are not recognized in every state, so it's important to consult with a local attorney. In addition, you can contact the Society for the Right to Die at 250 West 57th Street, New York, NY 10107. Their telephone number is (212) 246-6973.

The health care proxy should provide the substituted decision maker with guidance about when treatment should be withheld. However, the proxy document can also authorize the decision maker to continue treatment under specified circumstances. The document may also spell out the conditions under which the substituted decision maker's authority to make decisions is created. In other words, two doctors may need to certify that you are unable to make a medical decision before the proxy is effective.

The health care proxy is a broader and more flexible tool than a living will. However, the living will concept is more widely recognized. In states that recognize both concepts, it's probably a good idea to have both documents drafted to provide yourself with the greatest protection and flexibility.

32

EXCESS EARNINGS

When a retired couple is faced with the prospect of paying for the long-term care needs of an ill or frail spouse, the healthy spouse may be forced to return to work. Depending on the age and earning power of the well spouse, the couple may find themselves in the midst of a difficult "Catch-22." The well spouse may earn "too much" to qualify for their full Social Security benefits. Thus, earning more at a job to pay for long-term care expenses may result in total cash flow reductions due to the effect of earnings on Social Security benefits. This Key examines the problem of "excess earnings."

In order to collect Social Security "old age" benefits, you must be "retired." Congress has reasoned that if you work and earn more than a specified amount, you are not "retired" and, therefore, are subject to having some or all of your benefits eliminated. Congress does allow you some earnings before your benefits are jeopardized. The amount of allowable earnings depends on your age. If you are over 70, there is no limit on the amount you may earn and still collect your full benefit. If you are at least 65, but younger than 70, you may earn up to $9,720 in 1991 before your benefits are affected. If you are under 65, the limit is $7,080. The earnings limits are adjusted each year for inflation.

If you earn in excess of the limit, you must repay some or, potentially, all of the benefits you receive. If you are between 65 and 70, you must give up $1 of benefits for every $3 of earnings in excess of $9,720. If you are under 65, you must give up $1 for every $2 of earnings over $7,080. A special rule applies in the year in which you retire. In the initial retirement year, no matter how much is earned for the year, no benefits will be lost for any month in which you earn $810 or less ($590 for those under 65.)

For purposes of the retirement test, "earnings" are defined as "wages" earned as an employee or the "net earnings" of a self-employed person. The earnings must result from work performed after retirement. "In-kind" payments of goods or services in exchange for work are considered earnings. Retirement plan distributions, rents, capital gains, interest, dividends, and other investment related income *does not* count as "earnings" for this purpose. You are required to report estimated earnings in excess of the limits. Benefits are then adjusted to reflect the amount owed, based on the estimate. Actual earnings figures should be reported by April 15 of the following year. Further adjustments may then be made based on actual results.

Two examples illustrate how this rule works. Dr. Able is a 66-year-old retired surgeon who receives $1,000 per month in Social Security benefits. During 1991, Dr. Able earns $15,000 as a consultant. Dr. Able will have his benefit reduced by $1,760 (($15,000 − $9,720)/3.) Mr. Baker is a 63-year-old retired carpenter who receives $500 per month in Social Security benefits. During 1991, Mr. Baker earns a net of $9,000 for some cabinets he makes and sells. Mr. Baker's benefit will be reduced by $960 ((9,000 − 7,080)/2.)

33

REVERSE MORTGAGES

People over 65 control an estimated 19 percent of the wealth in this country, but much of their wealth is concentrated in the equity in their homes. With the rapidly rising cost of long-term care, some seniors may be tempted to tap the equity in their home to provide additional cash income. The so called *reverse mortgage* is a fairly new, novel way to turn the equity in your home into cash.

Reverse mortgages are mortgage loans that work backwards. Under a regular mortgage, the borrower sends a check to the lender every month to pay interest and reduce debt. With a reverse mortgage, the borrower receives a check every month from the lender and has his debt increase.

Reverse mortgages vary from lender to lender, but most have several characteristics in common. First, they are generally available only to senior citizens (the definition of who is a senior may vary from 62 to 70 years of age) who own and occupy their home with little or no debt. Next, the type of loan is either a term loan (with the term based on the life expectancy of the homeowner or a fixed time period) or a line of credit. The amount of the monthly payment depends on the term of the loan, interest rates, the value of the home, and the percentage of current equity eligible to be loaned out. With a line of credit arrangement, there is no monthly check; the senior merely taps the line of credit for cash whenever necessary. Generally, the loan is not repaid until the house is sold or at death. If you are the sole occupant of the home and are forced to seek long-term care in a nursing home or other facility, the payments under your reverse mortgage may stop, and the amounts paid to date must be repaid. This repayment probably will force the sale of the home.

The risks to the lender are obvious. With a loan based on life expectancy, more could be loaned than could be recovered at sale. There is no current cash inflow. Given these and other disadvantages, it is no wonder that lenders have not been flocking to offer reverse mortgages. The Federal Housing Administration has a loan guarantee program for reverse mortgages that may be expanded from 2,500 to 25,000 loans. If that occurs, we may see wider use of these loans.

The risk to the homeowner is also clear. The loan will eat away, and could wipe out, the value of the home. If the older person wanted to pass the home on to the next generation, that generation may be saddled with a sizeable debt. Reverse mortgages also carry with them many of the same charges associated with obtaining a conventional mortgage loan. In addition, monthly service fees may be assessed.

34

LEASEBACKS

A "leaseback" transaction is another device that, in the right circumstances, can help convert your home equity into cash. The cash can then be used to pay long-term care and other expenses. The technique is not without its pitfalls, however, and any leaseback transaction should be entered into only after consulting with an experienced real estate lawyer and carefully considering the transaction.

Leaseback transactions are fairly common in the business world. They are far less common among individuals dealing with personal use assets such as their home. In either case, the structure is the same. A leaseback is a two-step transaction. In the first step, you sell your home to a third party. In the second step, you enter into a lease agreement to rent the same house for a fixed period, typically life. Effectively you go from being an owner to being a renter without moving.

The investor in the home may be a third, unrelated party or it may be a relative. You should note that if the buyer/landlord is a relative, various tax considerations may become more important when the deal is structured. The price paid may have to be less than the value of your home to induce the buyer/landlord to give you a lifetime lease at a favorable rent. The sale of your home triggers the recognition for income tax purposes of any gain you have in the house. You may be able to use the $125,000 lifetime exclusion to avoid some or all of the tax on the gain (See Key 40).

The object and principal advantage of a leaseback transaction is to replace your home with cash that you can spend to offset long-term care or other expenses. If the buyer finances the purchase with a bank mortgage, you receive your cash in a lump sum. If you finance the sale, you receive cash payments every month, but you keep only the difference between the mortgage income and the rent expense. In addition, after the transaction, the buyer/landlord is typically responsible for maintenance, insurance, and property taxes on the home.

There are, however, numerous disadvantages to a leaseback transaction. First, finding a buyer willing to enter into such a transaction under terms that are appropriate may be difficult. Second, converting your home to cash converts an asset that may be exempt from Medicaid consideration into an asset that must be "spent down" to qualify for Medicaid. As a tenant you will be at the mercy, to a large extent, of a landlord who may turn out to be less than desirable. Your lease will give you some protection, but suing to enforce the lease may be both expensive and time consuming. The transaction will also be more expensive in terms of legal and, perhaps, some other fees than would a typical home sale contract. Finally, the tax considerations about the gain on the sale for you and the rental income for the buyer/landlord must be carefully addressed.

35

MEDICAL EXPENSE DEDUCTIONS

When planning for long-term care, it is important to consider the impact of income taxes. Knowing and understanding the income tax implications can provide a number of money-saving opportunities.

One of the first tax issues you should address is whether the expenses associated with long-term care qualify as medical expense deductions. If the expenses qualify as medical deductions, the taxable income, and therefore the income tax, of the nursing home resident may be substantially reduced or even eliminated. If you are supplying financial support for an aged parent or other relative, that individual may qualify as a dependent for income tax purposes (See Key 36). Under the tax laws, you can report the medical expenses of your dependents on your own return. You should consult your personal tax advisor about the application of any tax rule to your particular situation.

Medical expenses include any expenditure for the diagnosis, prevention, or treatment of disease or for treatment affecting a part of your body. Medical expenses do not include items of expense incurred primarily for personal reasons, such as a vacation to improve your state of mind, or expenditures to improve your general health. Naturally, there's plenty of room for disagreement with the IRS about whether an item qualifies as a medical expense. The IRS offers a booklet (Publication 502) that may help you and your tax advisor decide whether a particular expenditure is deductible.

If the primary reason for seeking long-term custodial care is medical, the cost of the nursing home, including meals and lodging, should be deductible as a medical expense. If you enter into a contract with a retirement community that allocates a portion of the initial fee to a promise of medical care, that portion of the fee is generally a medical expense. The cost of having a visiting nurse or other individual provide home health care should also be deductible.

The cost of medical insurance is deductible. Medicare premiums are also considered deductible medical expenses. The medical portion of your homeowners or automobile policy is not considered a medical expense; neither are life insurance or accidental death and dismemberment policies.

The cost of transportation to receive medical treatment is another deductible expense. You may even include the cost of having a nurse or someone else who travels with you if his or her presence is required because you need to have medication administered during the trip. You may calculate the actual cost of using your car to travel, or you may use a standard mileage rate. For purposes of medical expense deduction, the standard mileage rate is nine cents per mile. Under limited circumstances, you may include the nonhospital-related lodging costs of traveling away from home to receive medical care. You may not, however, deduct the cost of your meals.

If you must make capital improvements to your home because of your medical condition, these expenditures may be deductible. In addition to being medically necessary, the expenditure will only be deductible to the extent that it does not increase the value of your home. For example, because of a chronic and debilitating lung disorder, your doctor recommends that you install an expensive air filtration and cooling system to your home. The cost of the system is $5,000. You hired a competent appraiser to determine the value of your home before and after the improvement. The appraiser has concluded that the improvement increased the value of your home by $3,000. Thus, of the $5,000 total expenditure, only $2,000 is deductible. Note, however, that expenditures to remove architectural barriers (e.g., removing stairs to install ramps) are deductible in full by disabled persons. Expenditures for maintaining items installed in your home for medical purposes are also deductible.

Congress has imposed a "floor" on medical expense deductions. To be deductible, medical expenses must exceed 7.5 percent of your *adjusted gross income* (sometimes called AGI). Adjusted gross income equals your total income from wages, investments, capital gains and losses, rental income or loss, and any other source less deductions for IRA contributions, alimony payments, and certain other so-called "above the line" deductions. As a practical matter, your adjusted gross income appears on the last line of the front page of your IRS Form 1040.

36

DEPENDENTS

As children, we all start out dependent on our parents. When planning for long-term care we must recognize that we may wind up dependent on our children. For income tax purposes, whether you are considered the dependent of another can have a profound effect on deductions for personal exemptions and medical expense deductions.

Are you a "dependent" for income tax purposes? Five tests determine whether you will be considered the dependent of another: (1) the relationship test, (2) the citizenship test, (3) the joint return test, (4) the support test, and (5) the gross income test.

To meet the relationship test, the individual must be either one of a specified list of relatives or a full-time member of your houshold. To be exempt from the member of household requirement, the individual must be related in one of the following ways: (1) a child (including adopted children), grandchild or other lineal descendents; (2) a stepchild; (3) a sibling, half brother or sister, or step-brother or sister; (4) a parent, grandparent, or other lineal ancestor (not including foster parents); (5) stepparents; (6) aunts and uncles (but not great-aunts and great-uncles); (7) nieces and nephews (but not great-nieces and great-nephews); or (8) a father-in-law, mother-in-law, son-in-law, daughter-in-law, brother-in-law, or sister-in-law. If the individual is not related in one of these ways, then he or she must have been a member of your household for the entire year. Temporary absences from your household because of illness, vacation, or other similar reason does not disqualify a person from meeting the member-of-household requirement. Further, confinement to a nursing home for medical treatment for an unspecified period of time is considered temporary. An individual who dies during the year, but was a member of your household up until the time of death, meets the requirements.

The citizenship test requires that the individual must be either a United States citizen, a resident of the U.S., a resident of Canada, or a resident of Mexico. Residents of Puerto Rico must also be U.S. citizens. The joint return test is also fairly straightforward: You may not claim as your dependent someone who files a joint income tax return with another person.

The gross income test requires that the individual whom you would like to claim as a dependent must have gross income less than the amount of the personal exemption. The amount of the personal exemption for 1991 is $2,150. This amount is adjusted each year for inflation. Gross income includes all forms of *taxable* income whether received in cash, property, or otherwise. Gross income does not include Social Security benefits (if not otherwise taxable), tax-free municipal bond interest, gifts, or inheritances.

The final test is the support test, which in many respects, is the most confusing and complex. When computing support you must consider each potential dependent separately. If you want to claim another as your dependent, you must provide more than one-half of the support of that person for the year. Support, generally speaking, includes amounts expended for food, housing (including a nursing home), clothing, transportation, and medical care.

Certain items such as life insurance premiums, funeral expenses, and state and local income taxes are not included in support. In addition, although medical insurance and Medicare premiums may be included in support requirements, benefits paid under the policy or under Medicare are not included in support. Note that even if an item of income is excluded from "gross income" because it is not taxable, that same item of income is considered part of the support test if the cash is spent on support items. Finally, if income is received but not expended toward actually paying the support bills, that income is not counted toward the support test.

For example, Mabel, a widow and U.S. citizen, lives alone in an apartment. Her daughter, Connie, helps her mother financially. Mabel's total housing costs are $3,600 per year. Her food bill is $2,400 per year. She spends $1,500 annually on medical expenses. Her clothing costs are $500 each year. Mabel's total support is $8,000. Mabel's source of income is a $300 per month Social Security check. Connie provides the other $4,400 Mabel needs to live. Mabel meets the relationship, citizenship, and joint return test. She also meets the gross income test because her income of $3,600 in Social Security benefits is not taxable. Because Connie provides more than $4,000 in support, Mabel passes the support test as well.

Housing is an important element of the support test. The value of housing is computed based on the fair rental value of the dwelling. If the individual lives in his or her own home and the home is paid for, the rental value of the home is considered to be support provided by that individual.

If the individual lives in your home, the value of the housing support you are deemed to provide is equal to the fair rental value of the space in your home that the individual occupies. If the individual lives under your roof, you may compute your contribution to his or her support in the form of food and other household items by keeping a separate accounting of the receipts for these expenditures. Since this is often impractical, the IRS permits you to divide your household total for such things as food by the number of people in the household. You may then consider each individual's proportionate share of the expense as part of his or her support.

Consider another example. Harold and Margaret live with their son Steven, his wife, and their two children. A special rule applies to the support test if the individual resides in a nursing home sponsored by the state, a church, a fraternal organization, or other charitable organization. In that case, the subsidy provided by the nursing home for the care of the individual must be included as support provided by the individual. If the nursing home requires a lump sum advance payment for care based on life expectancy, then that amount will not count as support in the year of payment. Rather, you must divide the lump sum by the individual's life expectancy and include that fractional part in your support computation each year.

One benefit of having someone qualify as your dependent is that you may claim a personal exemption deduction for that individual. In 1991, each personal exemption is worth $2,150. The amount of tax you will save for each additional exemption depends on your tax bracket. For lower income taxpayers in the 15 percent bracket, each exemption saves $322.50 in federal income taxes in 1991. Middle income taxpayers in the 28 percent bracket save $602 for each exemption in 1990. Starting in 1991, upper income taxpayers will be in the 31 percent tax bracket and these taxpayers will save $666.50 for each exemption. However, under a new provision, very wealthy people (single people with adjusted gross incomes over $100,000 and married people with adjusted gross incomes over $150,000) will begin to lose the benefit of their personal exemptions.

The more important benefit of having someone requiring long-term care qualify as your dependent is your ability to deduct the medical expenses of your dependent. As discussed in Key 35, medical expenses are deductible to the extent that they exceed 7.5 percent of your adjusted gross income. The shear size of most annual long-term care bills greatly increases the likelihood of deductibility for all but the highest income taxpayers. If you are in the 28 percent marginal bracket, every $100 of deductible medical expenses over the 7.5 percent floor reduces your federal income taxes by $28. In effect, the government gives you a discount by lowering your income tax bill. Although this discount clearly does not eliminate the onerous burden of long-term care expenses, it may soften the blow.

37

MULTIPLE SUPPORT AGREEMENTS

Frequently, more than one family member provides for the support of a parent, grandparent, or other friend or relative requiring long-term care. Given the high cost of long-term care services, it is often impossible for any one family member to provide all the funds necessary to provide adequate care. If more than one person provides support, it's entirely possible that no one will provide more than one half of the support the elderly person requires. If no one provides more than half of the support, no one will be able to claim the elderly person as a dependent. Fortunately, Congress has provided a solution to this problem. The tax laws permit the use of a "multiple support agreement."

With a multiple support agreement one of the parties to the agreement may claim a dependency exemption every year. In addition, the person who is entitled to claim the dependency exemption may also include the medical expenses they paid for the dependent. You cannot claim as your medical expense deductions the medical expenses paid by the other parties to the agreement. Nor can you deduct medical expenses you paid if you were reimbursed by the other parties to the agreement. The other parties cannot deduct medical expenses paid until their turn to claim the dependency exemption.

There are four basic requirements for multiple support agreements. First, no one may contribute more than one half of the support. Second, those parties to the agreement must have been eligible to claim the individual as a dependent, except that they did not provide more than half of his or her support. Third, each person contributing support must contribute at least 10 percent of the total support. Finally, because only one member of the group may claim the individual as a dependent for each year, all other persons contributing more than 10 percent must file a written declaration stating that they will not claim the same individual as a dependent for the year. Multiple support agreements are made using IRS Form 2120.

Some examples will illustrate these rules. Consider Dorothy, a widow with three children—Anne, Bill, and Carl. Dorothy requires $10,000 per year in support. Anne provides $6,000, Bill and Carl provide $1,500 each, and Dorothy receives $1,000 in Social Security benefits that she uses for her own support. Anne, Bill, and Carl may not use a multiple support agreement because Anne provides more than one half of her mother's support. However, Anne may be able to claim Dorothy as a dependent, assuming the other tests are met.

Again assume the same facts, except that Anne provides $4,000 in support, Bill provides $4,500, and Carl provides $500. Given these facts, Anne and Bill may enter into a multiple support agreement, but Carl may not because he does not provide at least 10 percent of the support.

Finally, assume the same situation except that the three children provide $3,000 each in support. Now, all three may participate in the multiple support agreement. Multiple support agreements are available to spread tax benefits in situations when a family shares the burden of providing long-term care.

38

HEAD OF HOUSEHOLD STATUS

The burden of long-term care costs is often shared with adult children. If the adult child is single, a special tax filing status may be available. This status may provide tax brackets that are much more favorable than the rates normally applied to single taxpayers as well as a larger standard deduction. The special filing status is known as head of household.

To qualify as a head of household, you must be single and maintain the household where you and your child (grandchild or other lineal descendent) or any relative that may qualify as your dependent (See Key 36) reside. Your child or other lineal descendent need not qualify as your dependent for head of household purposes. However, if you are trying to qualify for head of household status because you maintain a household for your parents or other relative, that person must be able to qualify as your dependent. Individuals who qualify as your dependent because of a multiple support agreement (See Key 37) may not be used to qualify you for head of household status. If the individual you are using to qualify as a head of household dies during the year, you may still claim the status for the entire year.

To maintain a household, you must pay more than half the normal living expenses. These expenses generally include mortgage payments, rent, utilities, repairs, homeowner's/renter's insurance, maintenance, food, and similar items. Your home must be the principal place of residence for you and your child or other dependent. However, there is a special exception to this requirement for parents confined to a nursing home. You qualify for head of household status if you may claim one of your parents as a dependent and they reside with you for more than half the year. You may also qualify as a head of household if you maintain a separate household for your parents. For this purpose, a nursing home or home for the aged may qualify as a separate household.

A brief example will illustrate the benefits of the head of household filing status. Esther is 80 years old and lives with her 50-year-old daughter, Lorraine. Lorraine is recently divorced and has three grown children, none of whom live at home. Esther qualifies as Lorraine's dependent for income tax purposes. Lorraine pays all of the costs associated with maintaining the home. For 1991, Lorraine's adjusted gross income was $27,000. Had she filed as a single taxpayer with only one exemption and used the standard deduction her federal tax liability would have been about $3,361. Because Lorraine is entitled to claim her mother as a dependent, she may claim an additional $2,150 personal exemption. Lorraine also qualifies as a head of household. Using the head of household tax rates, the higher head of household standard and the additional personal exemption, her 1991 Federal tax liability is about $2,560. Proper use of the dependency exemption and the head of household filing status saved Lorraine about $1,800 in federal income taxes.

39

TAXING SOCIAL SECURITY BENEFITS

Many senior citizens rely heavily on their monthly Social Security checks to meet everyday living expenses. In recent years, Congress has begun to tax Social Security benefits in some cases. When faced with the expense of long-term care needs, you may wish to review your tax situation to see if anything can be done to reduce the taxation of your Social Security benefits. The taxes saved can then be put to a more productive use.

Social Security retirement, survivor, disability, and other benefits may be taxable. Tier 1 railroad retirement benefits are subject to the same rules. The taxable amount is the lesser of (1) one-half the benefit, or (2) one-half the excess of the taxpayer's income over a base amount. The key to understanding the taxation of these benefits is the computation of the income over the base amount. This computation begins with the taxpayer's adjusted gross income (AGI) (See Key 35) calculated before considering any additions due to the taxability of Social Security benefits.

AGI is modified by adding to it all tax-exempt interest, certain foreign source income items otherwise excluded from income, and U.S. savings bond interest excluded from income when used to pay the tuition costs of a dependent. The vast majority of taxpayers need only be concerned with tax-exempt interest—the interest paid on the municipal bonds issued by states, cities, towns, counties, and other municipalities. The result is termed *modified adjusted gross income*.

Next, add half of Social Security benefits to the modified AGI. This equals the taxpayer's "combined income." Deduct from the combined income figure the appropriate base amount. In the case of married individuals filing jointly, the base amount is $32,000. In the case of single individuals, the base amount is $25,000. For married people filing separately, the base amount is zero. Then multiply the difference by 50 percent. Compare this amount to half of Social Security benefits. The lesser of these two figures is included in the taxpayer's income.

For example, assume Charles and Diana are married and file a joint return. Their adjusted gross income for the year, before considering Social Security benefits, is $26,000, they have municipal income of $5,000 and receive total Social Security benefits of $12,000. The taxable amount of Social Security is computed as follows:

Adjusted Gross Income	$26,000
Municipal Interest	+ 5,000
Modified AGI	31,000
One-half of Social Security	+ 6,000
Combined Income	37,000
Base Amount	− 32,000
Excess	5,000

Because half of the excess over the base amount ($5,000 × 50 percent) is less than half of Social Security, the taxable amount of Social Security is $2,500.

Municipal bond income increases Social Security benefit taxation for those who have not reached the maximum taxable amount. However, income that is tax deferred (i.e., annuities) does not count in the computation. If you are receiving an annuity payment, the portion of the payment that counts as a nontaxable return of principal does not count in the computation.

40

SALES OF PERSONAL RESIDENCES

Seniors often sell their homes because they no longer want to spend the time necessary to maintain them. The home that seemed cramped with a family of two, three, or more growing chldren now seems empty. Senior citizens also sometimes relocate to sunny, warm areas such as Florida, Arizona, Texas, and California.

The sale of a residence may be necessary because of the demands of long-term care. The children of a widow or widower requiring long-term care may not wish to have the use of their parent's home. Under some circumstances, the sale of the home may be advisable to raise the capital necessary to pay for long-term care. This Key assumes that, after careful consideration of all available options, the sale of the home is the best alternative. Other than selling the home, some of the other options may include:

- leaseback
- taking in a boarder
- reverse mortgage
- giving the home to your children
- moving out and renting your home

Given that assumption, you should be aware of two special tax rules.

For any homeowner (regardless of age), no gain on the sale of a principal residence is recognized for tax purposes if the purchase price of a replacement home equals or exceeds the selling price, less certain expenses, of the old home. The replacement purchase must occur within the period starting two years before the sale of the old home and ending two years after the sale of the old home. If the purchase price of the replacement home is less than the selling price of the old, as adjusted, gain is recognized only to the extent that the selling price exceeds the purchase price. The cost of the replacement home is reduced by the amount of any gain not recognized. If a loss occurs on the sale of the old home, no deduction or offset against other capital gains is permitted.

An example illustrates these rules. John, age 50, buys a home for $60,000. Ten years later he sells the home for $100,000 less $6,000 in selling expenses for an adjusted selling price of $94,000. The sale produces a gain of $34,000. If John buys a new home within two years for at least $94,000, none of the gain will be recognized. However, if John buys a home for $70,000, then $24,000 of the gain ($94,000 − $70,000) will be recognized.

Taxpayers over age 55 receive an additional benefit. For these taxpayers, up to $125,000 of gain ($62,500 for married persons filing separately) may be permanently excluded from income. Several conditions must be met to qualify for the exclusion. First, the taxpayer *must* be over 55 when the sale occurs. Turning 55 in the year of sale does not qualify the seller for the exclusion. The taxpayer also must have lived in the home for three of the five years before the sale. A special rule applies to taxpayers confined to nursing homes. They may still qualify for the exclusion if they have lived in the home for at least *one* of the last five years. Remember, this is a once-in-a-lifetime exclusion!

For taxpayers who file a joint return, only one of them has to be over 55. For example, Harold and Wendy are 66 and 63, respectively, and they file their returns "married filing jointly." They purchased their home in 1965 for $30,000 and just sold it for $200,000, less $10,000 in selling expenses. They elect the $125,000 exclusion on their return. Therefore, the amount they realize on the sale is $65,000 ($200,000 − $10,000 − $125,000). The amount of gain they will recognize is $35,000 ($65,000 − $30,000).

The deferral and exclusion rules may be combined provided the requirements for each are met. For example, assume Harold and Wendy took the $190,000 net sales proceeds from the sale of their old home and headed to Florida to retire. If they buy a replacement home worth at least $65,000 within two years of the sale of the old home, no gain will be recognized. If they own the replacement home until the death of the survivor, their heirs will not have to pay capital gains taxes if they sell the property soon after the survivor's death.

41

DEPENDENT CARE CREDIT

Congress has provided another credit that may be beneficial to families trying to provide for the long-term care needs of an elderly parent, grandparent, or other relative. The "child and dependent care credit" can provide a maximum of $1,440 of income tax relief. The credit was originally conceived as a benefit for the many families in which both spouses work outside the home and some type of day care services must be provided. However, the credit is also available to families with two bread winners trying to cope with providing for the needs of a loved one who can no longer care for themselves.

To qualify for the credit, several criteria must be met. First, the individual for whose benefit the expenses are incurred must be: 1) a dependent under age 13, 2) a dependent unable to care for himself or herself, regardless of age, or 3) a spouse unable to take care of himself or herself. A special rule allows you to consider someone as your dependent for purposes of this credit, even if he or she has gross income over $2,150, provided the other four tests of dependency are met (See Key 36). The credit may be claimed for part of a year. For example, Gladys lives with her daughter Anne and son-in-law John. Gladys was fully able to care for herself until May 10 when she had a stroke. Since Anne and John both have full-time jobs, they have had to hire someone to provide Gladys with care while they both worked. The expenses incurred after May 10, the date of the stroke, may qualify for the credit.

The second test is whether you "maintain a home" in which you and at least one qualifying person lives. The qualifying person (i.e., the elderly loved one) need not live with you the entire year if the absence was attributable to a temporary absence (e.g., sickness, vacation) or death. To maintain the home, you must pay for the usual household expenses such as rent (or a mortgage payment), real estate taxes, utilities, insurance, and maintenance.

The third test requires that the expenses incurred to provide the care must have allowed you to work or to look for work. Your work cannot be volunteer in nature or work for which you receive only nominal compensation. If you are married, both spouses must be gainfully employed. Being a full-time student for at least five months during the year will count as "working" for purposes of this test. If you are married, however, only one spouse may be a student and still qualify for this credit.

The fourth test requires that the expenses be "work related." There are two types of work-related expenses. Expenses for household services include services such as cooking and cleaning, if they are required at least partly because you are providing for the elderly loved one. Household services may not include gardeners, chauffeurs, food, clothing, entertainment, and education. The other type of expenses includes those incurred to provide actual care for the elderly loved one. This care can be provided by someone brought into your home or at a "dependent care center." A dependent care center is a facility that provides care services for at least six people and receives compensation for providing the care. The center may be run either as a for-profit or not-for-profit facility. Finally, the center must comply with applicable laws. You may make payments to relatives that qualify as "work related" provided the relative is *not* someone for whom you claim a dependency exemption or is not your child under the age of 19.

Two limitations apply to the amount of work-related expenses that qualify for credit. First, the work-related expenses may not exceed your earnings from your work. If you are married, they may not exceed the earned income of the lower-paid spouse. Earned income includes wages, salaries, commissions, and other employer-provided earnings, as well as your net income if you are self-employed.

The other limitation is a dollar limitation, which depends on the number of individuals for whom the credit is claimed. If you incur work-related expenses to provide care for one qualifying person, the dollar limit is $2,400. If expenses are incurred for two or more persons, the dollar limit is $4,800.

A special rule may reduce these limits. Some employers provide an employee benefit sometimes called a "cafeteria plan." Cafeteria plans allow employees to choose among several different employee benefits, such as life insurance, disability insurance, and retirement plans, customizing their benefits to meet their needs. One of the benefits commonly included is a dependent care reimbursement program (also known as a dependent care assistance plan, flexible spending account, or some other name). Under a dependent care reimbursement program, the employee elects to have his or her salary reduced by a specified amount. The amount is deducted on a *before*-tax basis. The deferred compensation is placed in an account that the employee may draw upon to meet the expenses of dependent care. Under the special rule, the dollar limit must be reduced by the amount of compensation put into the account on a before-tax basis.

The credit is determined by multiplying the amount

of the eligible work-related dependent care expenses by a percentage. The percentage depends on your adjusted gross income (adjusted gross income is defined in Key 35). If your adjusted gross income is $10,000 or less, the appropriate percentage is 30 percent. The credit rate is reduced by 1 percent for every $2,000 by which your adjusted gross income exceeds $10,000, but the credit percentage will not fall below 20 percent. For example, Maureen and Jim incurred work-related expenses to care for Maureen's mother, Catherine. Maureen and Jim's adjusted gross income is $26,500. Their adjusted gross income exceeds $10,000 by $16,500. Dividing $16,500 by $2,000 equals 8.25. However, when making this calculation you must round up to the next whole number. Therefore, their credit rate is $30 - 9$ percent or 21 percent.

To claim the credit, you must be able to provide the name, address, and taxpayer identification (e.g., Social Security number) of the person or firm providing the care services. This information is entered on your Form 2441 (if you file a Form 1040) or on Schedule 1 (if you file a 1040A).

42

CREDIT FOR THE ELDERLY

Congress has provided some tax benefits for senior citizens who receive relatively small amounts of Social Security benefits or other nontaxable pensions. This relief is available for persons over 65 and certain totally and permanently disabled persons under 65. This Key focuses solely on the rules applicable to those over 65. This particular benefit is often underused in part because it is·so complex. The relief takes the form of a tax credit. The credit is available only to citizens or residents of the United States and the maximum amount is $1,125.

To compute the amount of the credit, you start with the appropriate "base amount." The base amount depends on your filing status. The appropriate base amounts are as follows:

Filing Status	Base Amount
Single, Head of Household	$5,000
Qualifying Widow(er)	
Married Filing Jointly	
(only one spouse over 65)	$5,000
Married Filing Jointly	
(both over 65)	$7,500
Married Filing Separately	
(and lived apart)	$3,750 ·

The next step in computing the credit is to reduce the base amount by 1) the amount of any nontaxable Social Security (See Key 39) or other nontaxable pensions and 2) by an amount computed with reference to your adjusted gross income.

The reduction of the base amount that depends on your adjusted gross income requires a bit of explanation. In typical IRS fashion, this amount has a technical name that is not particularly helpful—excess adjusted gross income. To compute the adjustment you begin with your adjusted gross income (See Key 35). Adjusted gross income is then reduced by an amount that depends on your filing status, as shown below:

Filing Status	Amount
Single, Head of Household, Qualifying Widow(er)	$ 7,500
Married filing jointly	$10,000
Married filing separately	$ 5,000

Finally, subtract the amount from the table from your adjusted gross income and then divide the difference by two. After deducting the nontaxable Social Security and the excess adjusted gross income from the base amount, multiply the difference by 15 percent to arrive at the credit.

This complex credit system requires an example. Consider the case of Edgar and his wife Agnes who are both 68-year-old U.S. citizens and file a joint return. They receive $3,000 per year in Social Security, $2,000 per year in taxable interest, and a $9,000 per year fully taxable pension. Edgar and Agnes would compute their credit for the elderly as follows:

Step 1: Determine the base amount. Because both Edgar and Agnes are over 65, the appropriate base amount is $7,500.

Step 2: Determine the total amount of nontaxable Social Security and other nontaxable pensions. Their entire $3,000 Social Security benefit is nontaxable.

Step 3: Determine the amount of adjusted gross income. Edgar and Agnes' adjusted gross income (assuming no other taxable transactions) equals the sum of their taxable interest and taxable pension, or $11,000.

Step 4: Determine the appropriate figure for calculating the excess adjusted gross income. Because Edgar and Agnes are married and file jointly, this figure is $10,000.

Step 5: Subtract the amount determined in Step 4 from adjusted gross income. In this case, subtract $10,000 from $11,000 to arrive at $1,000.

Step 6: Divide the difference determined in Step 5 by two. In this case, $1,000 divided by two is $500.

Step 7: Deduct from the base amount determined in Step 1, the amount of nontaxable Social Security from Step 2 and the amount calculated in Step 6. In this case, start with $7,500 and subtract $3,000 and $500 for a net difference of $4,000.

Step 8: Multiply the amount calculated in Step 7 by 15 percent to determine the credit. Edgar and Agnes will receive a credit of $600 ($4,000 × 15 percent). By the way, if the amount of the credit calculated exceeds the amount of your tax, the government does *not* refund the difference.

The credit for the elderly is claimed using IRS Schedule R. This schedule must be filed with Form 1040. The IRS will calculate the amount of the credit for you. To have the IRS calculate the credit write "CFE" on the line next to the entry for the credit on Form 1040. Also attach Schedule R with your name(s), Social Security number(s), age(s), and filing status filled in.

43

GIFT TAXES

Planning for long-term care should occur in conjunction with planning for the other financial aspects of your life. Estate planning considerations are among the factors you need to consider in your overall financial plan. Gifts of money or assets to family and friends may be an important part of your estate plan. Gifts may also be beneficial within the context of long-term care planning. As discussed in Key 19, a pattern of gift giving designed to comply with applicable regulations may allow you to qualify for Medicaid, so it is worthwhile to review briefly some of the tax aspects of making a gift.

Both the United States and almost all state governments impose death taxes. In addition, the United States and some states impose taxes on lifetime gifts. This Key concentrates on the federal gift and estate tax implications of making a gift. Consult your tax advisor to determine if your state imposes a gift tax.

The federal estate and gift tax systems have been "unified" for about a decade. That means that many of the rules that apply to the gift tax also apply to the estate tax. For example, there is an unlimited gift and estate deduction for gifts to charities. Under our system of gift and estate taxation, each person may transfer up to $600,000 in assets to other people without paying any gift or estate taxes. A married couple, provided they take the proper estate planning steps, may pass up to $1.2 million to their loved ones without tax. The $600,000 is really a translation of the so-called "unified credit." Under unified credit, each person receives a

135

credit of $192,800 against gift and estate taxes. Remember, a tax credit is a dollar-for-dollar reduction of the tax. Using the estate and gift tax tables, a $192,800 credit is the equivalent of a transfer of $600,000 in property.

In addition to the $600,000 lifetime exclusion, you may give a gift of $10,000 in value per year to as many people as you would like without incurring any gift tax, without using up any of your lifetime $600,000 exclusion, and without the need to file a gift tax return. Married couples may give up to $20,000 to any one person without gift tax costs, but married couples giving more than $10,000 may have to file a special short form gift tax return. No tax will be due and the form is quite simple to prepare.

To qualify for the $10,000 per year "annual exclusion," the gift must be a "present interest." Present interest is a legal term that means the person receiving the gift must be able to enjoy at least some of its benefits immediately. Outright gifts to adults qualify as present interests. You may wish to use some form of trust when making your gift to ensure that the gift is used in the way you intended. Gifts to trusts may or may not qualify as present interests, depending on the terms of the trust. Consult with your attorney before embarking on any gift-giving strategy to explore both the tax and long-term care planning aspects of your planned gifts.

To the extent that gifts exceed $10,000 per year per person, you begin to "use up" some of your $600,000. Technically, what occurs is that the value of your gift over $10,000 is included in your estate for federal estate tax purposes. The gift, however, is included in the estate at its date of gift (not date of death) value. This can be a powerful advantage.

Consider Maude's situation. Maude, a widow, had an estate of $750,000. Although in good health, Maude decided to begin a program of giving gifts to her son John to reduce her estate tax burden and increase the likelihood that she may someday be able to qualify for Medicaid or a similar program. Included among Maude's assets was a parcel of unimproved, raw land having a current value of $100,000. Maude gave this parcel to her son and filed a gift tax return showing the value of the land as $100,000. From this amount, the $10,000 annual exclusion was deducted. Maude had made a $90,000 "taxable gift" and had "used up" a portion of her $600,000 lifetime exclusion. However, she was not required to pay any gift taxes.

Maude died four years after making the gift. At the time of her death, her estate was worth $650,000. The land, however, had appreciated due to the expansion of her hometown to a value of $300,000. Nonetheless, for federal estate tax purposes, the amount of the gift included in her estate was only $90,000, the value of the taxable gift at the time it was made. Taxable gifts of appreciating property can be a powerful tool to reduce estate taxes and may be appropriate as part of a strategy when planning for long-term care.

Generally, assets may be transferred in any amount between husband and wife without gift or estate tax consequences. However, if you want to give your spouse rights to property that some day may terminate, special care must be taken to structure the transfer to minimize the tax impact. For example, perhaps you want to transfer $100,000 to a trust that will benefit your second wife during her life, but at her death the balance of the trust is to be paid to your children from your first marriage. This trust must be carefully drafted according to certain special rules to avoid making it a taxable transfer.

Another special rule must be considered if your spouse is not a U.S. citizen. If you are transferring assets to a noncitizen spouse, that spouse is *not* entitled to receive an unlimited amount of wealth without tax consequences. Rather, you may only transfer up to $100,000 per year to a noncitizen spouse. In addition, further special rules apply to transfers at death to a noncitizen spouse.

Gifts are valued for tax purposes at their fair market value at the time of the gift. Valuing gifts of marketable stocks, bonds, mutual funds, and other publicly traded securities is fairly simple. The gift tax value of these items is based on their published prices on the day of the gift. Other assets, such as real estate and stock in family corporations, are somewhat more difficult to value. For assets with no public market, the gift tax value is generally based on an independent appraisal by a qualified, expert appraiser. Gifts of life insurance contracts are valued using a special computation that will be provided by your insurance company upon request.

44

GIFT TAX EXCLUSION FOR MEDICAL EXPENSES

Key 43 dealt with some general gift tax issues. The $10,000 annual gift tax exclusion can be a useful tool when planning for long-term care, as well as general estate planning. A special gift tax rule may have particular application in the long-term care arena, particularly when children are providing support for their parents.

When the gifts are made for the payment of medical expenses, there is an *unlimited* gift tax exclusion. There is no requirement that the donor be related in any way to the recipient. If one close friend wants to pay the medical expenses of the other friend, the payment will qualify for the unlimited exclusion. The expense must qualify as a medical expense deduction. For more information on what qualifies as a deductible medical expense see Key 35. The payment also must be made directly to the provider of the medical care. The parent or other recipient of the gift need not be a dependent of the child or other donor to qualify for this exclusion. The special exclusion does not apply if the medical expenses are reimbursed by insurance.

This gift tax exclusion may, in certain circumstances, allow children to pay the medical expenses of their parents in a taxwise manner. For example, Sadie is 75 years old and is recovering from an illness. Her doctor has suggested that she spend a few months in a nursing home receiving custodial care while she regains her strength. There is every reason to believe that Sadie will be able to return to her apartment after her stay in the nursing home. Sadie's income is not sufficient to cover the cost of the nursing home. Medicare will not cover the cost and neither will her Medigap policy. Sadie owns several hundred shares of a publicly traded stock that pays a very low dividend. She could sell some of her shares to pay the nursing home, but the sale would result in a sizeable gain. Besides, Sadie promised her late husband, Herman, that she would pass the stock to their sons, Martin and Elliot. Martin and Elliot have both been financially successful. Martin is a doctor with a thriving practice. Elliot owns his own business. They can afford to pay the roughly $30,000 they think it will cost for their mother's uninsured medical expenses. If they do, they will not have any gift tax costs, and they will be able to preserve the block of stock in their mother's name.

QUESTIONS AND ANSWERS

Q. I hate the thought of winding up in a nursing home. Are there any alternatives?

A. Yes, depending on your physical condition. For example, you may be able to utilize visiting nurses, "meals on wheels" programs, and/or a nearby child or other loved one to help you stay right in your own home. Or, you may be able to share your home or another's home to get the help you need. Other shared living arrangements and continuing care retirement communities are among the options that can be explored.

Q. What are the different types of nursing homes?

A. There are basically three types of nursing homes. The differences between them relate to the level of care that they provide. *Skilled nursing facilities* provide the highest level of care with around-the-clock nurses and doctors on staff. *Intermediate care facilities* also provide registered nursing services, but their care is not necessarily needed around-the-clock. *Residential care facilities* provide custodial care. Custodial care consists of assistance with the activities of daily life (i.e. eating, dressing, and so on).

Q. If I need to go into a nursing home, how much will it cost?

A. That depends on the location of the home and the level of care you need. Urban areas tend to be more expensive than rural areas. Skilled care is more expensive than custodial care. The broad national average for custodial care is between $22,000 and $30,000 per year.

Q. Doesn't Medicare cover nursing home expenses?

A. Probably not. Medicare Part A does provide some benefits for confinements in skilled nursing facilities. Medicare pays a benefit for 100 days per benefit period. For the first 20 days, Medicare pays 100 percent of the approved amount. For the next 80 days, Medicare pays the cost in excess of $78.50. In order to qualify for these benefits you must have had at least a three-day stay in a hospital prior to the nursing home and you must be admitted to the nursing home within 30 days of being discharged from the hospital.

Q. What is Medicaid?

A. Medicaid is a joint program between the federal government and the various state governments. It is designed to provide health care benefits for poor people.

Q. Does Medicaid cover custodial nursing home care?

A. Yes. However, you must first be eligible for Medicaid. That may mean you will have to spend yourself into poverty in order to qualify. You must also stay in a Medicaid approved nursing home.

Q. Is it legal to arrange your financial affairs in order to qualify for Medicaid?

A. Yes, provided you follow the rules that apply in your state. Medicaid rules are highly complex and vary from state to state. If you are going to try to qualify for Medicaid, it pays to have the help of an attorney familiar with the laws of your state.

Q. Can't I just give my assets to my spouse or my children to make myself poor enough for Medicaid?

A. Not really. The assets of married people are combined for Medicaid eligibility purposes, so transferring assets to a spouse is not an effective strategy. Giving assets away to children or any other third party may be somewhat more successful. However, any gift within 30 months of going into the nursing home and applying for benefits may eliminate Medicaid benefits for a certain period of time. Benefits will be denied for the shorter of 30 months or the number of months determined by dividing the value of the asset(s) transferred by the average monthly cost of a local nursing home.

Q. Will my health insurance or Medicare supplement policy cover custodial care in a nursing home?
A. Generally, the answer is no, unless you have an unusual policy that provides some nursing home benefits.

Q. Does any type of insurance policy cover long-term care?
A. Yes. There are two general types of policies that are available. Traditional long-term care insurance pays a daily benefit, within policy limits, for every day you are in the nursing home. A new feature, called a living benefit, is available on some cash value life insurance policies that allows you to receive part of the "death" benefit, within policy limits, while confined in a nursing home. Both types of policies should be reviewed carefully to determine if they are right for you.

Q. What is a guardianship proceeding?
A. A guardianship proceeding involves a judge declaring, after hearing appropriate evidence, that you are legally incompetent, and then appointing a guardian for you. A guardian is an individual who is appointed by a court to make financial, health, and other decisions for you after you have been declared incompetent.

Q. Is there any way to avoid a guardianship proceeding?

A. Yes, there are a couple of strategies you can use to reduce or eliminate the chance of ever needing a guardian. A *revocable living trust* is a legal agreement under which you may appoint a trustee to act in your behalf to manage the assets owned by the trust. Another tool you can use is a durable power of attorney. A *durable power of attorney* allows you to grant another person to manage your financial affairs in the event you no longer can do it yourself. There are advantages and disadvantages to both methods that should be explored with an experienced attorney.

Q. Who will make my health care decisions if I can't make them for myself?

A. Depending on the circumstances, a guardian may have to be appointed to make those decisions. It may be possible to avoid a guardian for health-care decisions by using a living will or a health care proxy. Generally, a *living will* is a legal document in which you describe the kind of treatment you would like to receive in the event you are faced with a life threatening condition and you cannot speak for yourself. A *health care proxy* allows you to appoint someone else, a spouse or other family member, to make health-care decisions for you. The rules for living wills and health care proxies vary from state to state so, again, it pays to consult an attorney in your area.

Q. Are nursing home expenses deductible on my income tax return?

A. If you are in the nursing home for medical reasons, your expenses are generally deductible for income tax purposes. Medically necessary home health-care expenditures are also generally deductible. Medical expenses are deductible to the extent that total expenses exceed 7.5 percent of your adjusted gross income.

Q. My sister and I help support my mother who is eighty-five years old and needs home health care. Am I entitled to any tax benefits?

A. Yes, there are some possible benefits. If you pay for more than one half of her support and if the other four criteria are met (See Key 36), you may be able to claim your mother as a dependent. That will entitle you to claim a $2,150 (in 1990) personal exemption. It will also permit you to include the medical expenses you pay in your itemized deductions. If you pay less than half of her support but together with your sister you meet the criteria discussed in Key 37, you may be able to use a multiple support agreement. A *multiple support agreement* will allow you and your sister to take turns claiming your mother as a dependent and claiming the medical expenses each of you pays.

Q. I am having trouble getting around and I'd like to have one of my three children as a joint owner of all my bank accounts so that I can be taken care of in case anything happens to me. Does this make sense?

A. What you propose is very common and may be appropriate in a limited number of cases, but the strategy has some very significant drawbacks. First, it is possible, depending on the law of your state and the terms of the bank account, that merely adding a child to a joint account may not eliminate the need for a guardian if you become infirm. Second, as unpleasant as this may seem, there have been numerous cases of children and other close relatives converting the funds in a joint account for their own use. There may also be unintended estate, gift, and income tax implications. Finally, if the child you name as joint owner survives you, that child is under no obligation to share any of the proceeds of the account with his or her siblings. The use of a durable power of attorney or revocable living trust may be a better solution.

GLOSSARY

Activity of daily living a term that includes eating, dressing, bathing, walking, getting into and out of a chair or bed, and toileting. Individuals requiring long-term custodial care have difficulty doing these activities without assistance.

Adult day care facility a facility available in many communities. It is similar to child day care facilities, but is intended for those receiving long-term custodial care in a home. It allows the care giver to pursue a career outside of the home or provides the care giver with an opportunity for a respite from the rigors of daily care.

Attorney-in-fact the individual empowered to act in behalf of another according to the terms of a power of attorney or durable power of attorney.

Board and care home a type of shared living arrangement. Under a typical board and care arrangement, a home's owner provides a room, meals, and some other basic services in exchange for a monthly rental. A board and care home is typically occupied by the owner and a small group of senior citizens who are able to engage in the activities of daily living but desire the companionship and other benefits of group living.

Community spouse a Medicaid term for the spouse who is not confined to a nursing home and not applying for Medicaid.

Congregate living center an apartment-like facility in which independent senior citizens have their own apartment and may receive, in addition, hotel-like services. Many of these communities were constructed with government subsidies.

Durable power of attorney a legal device that permits an individual to designate a third person to act in his or her behalf. Durable powers of attorney are useful devices for the management of one's financial affairs in the event of incapacity. They are a tool to avoid a guardianship proceeding.

ECHO unit an acronym for *E*lder *C*ottage *H*ousing *O*pportunity. Generally it describes a temporary structure erected on an existing homesite to provide living space for an elderly person whose nearby relatives provide care. In a loose sense, it may also refer to any modification of an existing home to make room for an elderly relative requiring care.

Financial planning the disciplined process of making financial decisions that involves gathering information, setting objectives, evaluating problems and alternative solutions, creating a written plan of action, implementing the plan, and reviewing and revising the plan.

Grantor the legal term for the person who establishes a trust. The terms settlor and trustor are substituted for grantor in some states.

Group home a form of shared living in which a small to medium size group of people share a home and the responsibilities for maintaining the home and household chores. The home may be sponsored by a charitable organization.

Guardian the individual appointed by a court to make decisions for someone who has been declared legally incompetent. *Guardian of the person* refers to a guardian who may make health related and similar decisions. *Guardian of the estate* refers to a guardian who is responsible for financial decisions. Similar terms are conservator and committee.

Guardianship proceeding the legal proceeding required to have someone declared legally incompetent to make his or her own decisions and to appoint a guardian(s) as the substituted decision maker.

Health care proxy a legal device permitted in some states allowing you to designate another to make your health-care decisions in the event you are unable. Also called durable power of attorney for health care.

Health Maintenance Organization (HMO) an organization that allows members to receive medical services from participating providers for a flat periodic fee. HMOs typically have no or very low deductible and co-payment provisions.

Hospice a philosophy of treatment for terminally ill patients. Hospice programs are designed to treat and help relieve the physical and emotional pain of patients who are terminal. They provide medical care to the patient and counseling to the patient and his or her family.

Intermediate Care Facility (ICF) a type of nursing home that provides care that is more extensive than that provided in a residential care facility but less involved than the care provided in a skilled nursing facility. Patients in an intermediate care facility may require, among other things, the care of a registered nurse on a less than 24-hour basis.

Joint tenancy a form of co-ownership between two or more people who own an item of real or personal property. The joint tenants have equal rights to the asset during their lives. At the death of each joint tenant, the deceased's interest passes automatically to the survivor. The ultimate disposition of the asset is controlled by the last to die. Also called joint tenancy with rights of survivorship.

Leaseback an arrangement under which a home owner sells his or her home to a third party and then immediately enters into a long-term lease with the buyer. A leaseback allows a home owner to receive his or her equity in the home without having to give up the right to live in the home.

Living benefits life insurance a form of cash value life insurance that permits a policyholder to access some or all of the death benefit during life if certain conditions are met. Some living benefits policies provide a monthly benefit, under policy conditions, if the policyholder is confined to a nursing home.

Living will a legal device in which you state the type of care you would like to receive in the event you are faced with a life-threatening condition and are unable to make medical decisions for yourself.

Long-term care insurance a general term for a type of indemnity insurance policy that promises to pay the owner of the policy a daily benefit, within policy terms, for home health care and/or nursing home confinements. Long-term care policies vary widely in cost and features and must be evaluated carefully.

Medicaid a welfare program jointly administered by the federal and state governments to provide health care to poor people . Medicaid will provide benefits for eligible individuals who require long-term custodial care.

Medicare the principal health care program sponsored by the federal government to provide health care insurance for senior citizens. Although providing extensive benefits for hospital, outpatient, and doctor care, Medicare provides very few benefits for those requiring long-term custodial care.

Medigap insurance the popular name for those health insurance policies designed to cover the deductible, co-payments, and other "gaps" that exist under the Medicare program. Generally, Medigap policies do not provide benefits for long-term care. Medigap policies are also called Medicare supplement policies.

Multiple support agreement an agreement under the tax laws that allows several family members to take turns claiming, in the typical case, an elderly parent or other relative as dependent. If the criteria are met, parties to the agreement alternate claiming the personal exemption and medical expense deductions of the dependent relative.

Residential Care Facility (RCF) a type of nursing home that provides custodial care. Custodial care involves assistance with the activities of daily living. Most of the services can be provided by licensed practical nurses and other less highly trained health care providers. The care provided in a residential care facility is the crux of the problem of long-term care.

Reverse mortgage a form of loan arrangement under which an elderly home owner may access the equity in his or her home. Reverse mortgages generally take one of two forms. There may be a line of credit against the home that the home owner taps by writing a check. The other form involves the home owner receiving a regular check from the lender. Each check increases the amount of the debt against the home.

Revocable living trust A type of trust that permits the grantor to change any or all of the terms of the trust at any time. The trust is established during the life of the grantor. A living trust is also called an *inter vivos* trust. Revocable living trusts are useful tools to help manage your financial affairs in the event you become incapacitated.

Skilled Nursing Facility (SNF) a facility that provides the highest level of nursing home care. Patients at these facilities receive, among other things, around-the-clock care by registered nurses. Medicare provides some benefits for those confined to this type of facility.

Trust a legal agreement under which one person (the grantor, settlor, or trustor) transfers legal title to property to the trustee to be managed and distributed to the beneficiaries according to the instructions of the grantor.

Trustee the individual(s) or corporation who manages and distributes assets under the terms of a trust.

APPENDIX A
LONG-TERM CARE
INSURANCE CHECKLIST

	Policy #1	Policy #2
Rated A or A + by Best's	Yes/No	Yes/No
Guaranteed renewable	Yes/No	Yes/No
Fixed premium	Yes/No	Yes/No
Covers all levels of care	Yes/No	Yes/No
Covers all types of facilities	Yes/No	Yes/No
Home health care benefits	Yes/No	Yes/No
Benefit paid in excess of actual cost	Yes/No	Yes/No
Covers organic brain disorders (e.g., Alzheimer's)	Yes/No	Yes/No
Preexisting conditions excluded	Yes/No	Yes/No
If yes, for how long?	___ months	___ months
Prior hospitalization required	Yes/No	Yes/No
Prior skilled/intermediate nursing care required	Yes/No	Yes/No
Inflation protection	Yes/No	Yes/No

Activity of daily living or doctor's certification	_____	_____
Daily benefit—nursing home	$_____	$_____
Daily benefit—home care	$_____	$_____
Elimination period	_____days	_____days
Benefits payable for	_____years/life	_____years/life
Annual premium	$_____	$_____

APPENDIX B
LIST OF AGENCIES
FOR THE ELDERLY

State Government Agencies
Alabama
Commission on Aging
Second Floor, 136 Catoma Street
Montgomery, AL 36130   (205) 242-5743

Alaska
Older Alaskans Commission
Department of Administration, Pouch C
Juneau, AK 99811   (907) 465-3250

Arizona
Aging and Adult Administration
Department of Economic Security,
P.O. Box 6123
Phoenix, AZ 85005   (602) 542-4446

Arkansas
Office on Aging and Adult Services
Department of Human Services
Donaghey Building,
7th and Main Streets
Little Rock, AR 72201   (501) 682-2441

California
Department on Aging
1600 K Street
Sacramento, CA 95814   (916) 322-5290

Colorado

Division of Aging and Adult Services
Department of Social Services Building
1575 Sherman Street–10th floor
Denver, CO 80203 (303) 866-3851

Connecticut

Department on Aging
175 Main Street
Hartford, CT 06106 (203) 566-3238

Delaware

Division of Aging
Department of Health and Social Services
1901 N. DuPont Highway
New Castle, DE 19720 (302) 421-6139

District of Columbia

Long-Term Care Administration
Department of Human Services
Commission of Public Health
1660 L Street, N.W.
Washington, D.C. 20036 (202) 673-3597

Office of Aging
1424 K Street, N.W.
Washington, D.C. 20005 (202) 724-5622

Florida

Aging and Adult Services Program Office
Department of Health and Rehabilitative Services
1321 Winewood Boulevard
Tallahassee, FL 32301 (904) 488-8922

Georgia

Office of Aging
Georgia Department of Human Resources
878 Peachtree Street, N.E. Room 632
Atlanta, GA 30309 (404) 894-2022

Guam

Guam Public Health and Social Services
Government of Guam
Agana, Guam 96910

Hawaii

Executive Office on Aging
335 Merchant Street, Room 241
Honolulu, HI 96813   (808) 548-2593

Idaho

Idaho Office on Aging
Statehouse, Room 108
700 West State Street
Boise, ID 83720   (208) 334-3833

Illinois

Department on Aging
421 East Capitol Avenue
Springfield, IL 62701   (217) 785-3356

Indiana

Division of Aging
150 W. Market St. P.O. Box 7083
Indianapolis, IN 46207-7083   (317) 232-7020

Iowa

Department of Elder Affairs
Jewett Building, Suite 236
914 Grand
Des Moines, IA 50319   (515) 281-5187

Kansas

Department on Aging
915 S.W. Harrison
Topeka, KS 66612-1500   (913) 296-4986

Kentucky

Division for Aging Services
Department for Social Services
Cabinet for Human Resources,
275 East Main Street
Frankfort, KY 40621   (502) 564-6930

Louisiana

Governor's Office of Elderly Affairs
P.O. Box 80374
Baton Rouge, LA 70806   (504) 925-1700

Maine

Bureau of Maine's Elderly
Department of Human Services,
State House Station 11
Augusta, ME 04333   (207) 289-2561

Maryland

Maryland Office on Aging
301 West Preston Street
Baltimore, MD 21201   (301) 225-1102

Massachusetts

Department of Elder Affairs
38 Chauncey Street
Boston, MA 02111   (617) 727-7750

Michigan

Office of Services to the Aging
611 W. Ottawa, 3rd floor
Lansing, MI 48933   (517) 373-7876

Minnesota

Minnesota Board on Aging
444 Lafayette Rd.
St. Paul, MN 55155-3843   (612) 296-2770

Mississippi

Council on Aging
421 West Pascagoula
Jackson, MS 39203   (601) 949-2070

Missouri

Division of Aging
Department of Social Services,
P.O. Box 1337
Jefferson City, MO 65102   (314) 751-3082

Montana

Montana Governor's Office on Aging
Capitol Station
Helena, MT 59620   (406) 444-3311

Nebraska

Department of Aging
301 Centennial Mall South,
P.O. Box 95044
Lincoln, NE 68509   (402) 471-2306

Nevada

Division for Aging Services
1665 Hot Springs Rd., Suite 158
Carson City, NV 89710   (702) 687-4210

New Hampshire

Division of Elderly and Adult Services
6 Hazen Drive
Concord, NH 03301   (603) 271-3610

New Jersey

Department of Community Affairs
Division on Aging
South Broad and Front Streets, CN 807
Trenton, NJ 08625   (609) 292-4833

New Mexico

State Agency on Aging
224 E. Palace Ave., 4th floor
Sante Fe, NM 87503 (505) 827-7640

New York

New York State Office for the Aging
Empire State Plaza, Agency Building 2
Albany, NY 12223 (518) 474-4425

North Carolina

Department of Human Resources
Division on Aging
Caller Box Number 29531
693 Palmer Drive
Raleigh, NC 27626 (919) 733-3983

North Dakota

Aging Services
600 E. Boulevard Ave.
Bismarck, ND 58505-0250 (701) 224-2577

Ohio

Department of Aging
50 West Broad Street, 9th floor
Columbus, OH 43266 (614) 466-5500

Oklahoma

Oklahoma Special Unit on Aging
Department of Human Services
P.O. Box 25352
Oklahoma City, OK 73125 (405) 521-2281

Oregon

Senior Services Division
313 Public Service Building
Salem, OR 97310 (503) 378-4728

Pennsylvania

Department of Aging
Barto Building,
231 State Street
Harrisburg, PA 17101   (717) 783-1550

Puerto Rico

Department of Health
Building A,
Call Box 70184
San Juan, PR 00936 (809) 766-1616 or (809) 766-2200

Rhode Island

Department of Elderly Affairs
160 Pine Street
Providence, RI 02903   (401) 277-2894

South Carolina

Commission on Aging
400 Arbor Lake Dr., Suite B-500
Columbia, SC 29201   (803) 734-3203

South Dakota

Office of Adult Services and Aging
Department of Social Services
Kneip Building,
700 Governor's Drive
Pierre, SD 57501   (605) 773-3656

Tennessee

Commission on Aging
706 Church Street, Suite 201
Nashville, TN 37243-0860   (615) 741-2056

Texas
Texas Department on Aging
1949 South I.H. 35
Austin, TX 78711   (512) 444-2727

Utah
Division of Aging
120 North 200 West
Salt Lake City, UT 84103   (801) 538-3910

Vermont
Office on Aging
103 South Main
Waterbury, VT 05671-2301   (802) 241-2400

Virginia
Virginia Department for Aging
700 East Franklin Street, 10th floor
Richmond, VA 23219   (804) 225-2271

Washington
Aging and Adult Services
Department of Social and Health Services
12th and Franklin Mail Stop OB-44A
Olympia, WA 98504   (206) 586-3768

West Virginia
Commission on Aging
State Capitol, Holly Grove
Charleston, WV 25305   (304) 348-3317

Wisconsin
Bureau of Aging
217 South Hamilton
Madison, WI 53707   (608) 266-2536

Wyoming
Commission on Aging
Hathaway Building
Cheyenne, WY 82002   (307) 777-7986

Federal Agencies

Division of Disability, Aging, and Long-term Care
U.S. Department of Health and Human Services
200 Independence Avenue, S.W.
Washington, D.C. 20201   (202) 245-6172

Administration on Aging
U.S. Department of Health and Human Services
330 Independence Avenue, S.W.
Washington, D.C. 20201   (202) 245-0724

Health Care Financing Administration
Division of Medicare Eligibility Policy
U.S. Department of Health and Human Services
East High Rise Building, 6325 Security Boulevard
Baltimore, MD 21207   (301) 966-4472
Division of Medicaid Eligibility Policy (301) 966-4452

Health Care Financing Administration
Division of Long Term Care Experiments
U.S. Department of Health and Human Services
Oak Meadows Building
6340 Security Boulevard
Baltimore, MD 21207   (301) 966-6649

National Institute on Aging
9000 Rockville Pike
Rockville, MD 20892   (301) 496-9265

Social Security Administration
6401 Security Boulevard
Baltimore, MD 21235   (301) 594-6660

Veterans Administration
Assistant Chief Medical Director for Geriatrics and
Extended Care
810 Vermont Avenue, N.W.
Washington, D.C. 20420   (202) 233-3781

National Associations and Organizations

American Association of Homes for the Aging
(AAHA)
1129 20th Street, N.W., Suite 400
Washington, D.C. 20036   (202) 296-5960

American Association of Retired Persons (AARP)
1909 K Street, N.W.
Washington, D.C. 20049   (202) 872-4700

American Bar Association Commission on Legal
Problems for the Elderly
1800 M Street, N.W.
Washington, D.C. 20036   (202) 331-2297

American Health Care Association
1201 L Street, N.W.
Washington, D.C. 20005   (202) 898-2842

American Society on Aging
833 Market Street
San Francisco, CA 94103   (415) 543-2617

Health Insurance Association of America
1025 Connecticut Avenue, N.W., Suite 1200
Washington, D.C. 20036   (202) 223-7780

Legal Services for the Elderly
132 West 43rd Street, 3rd Floor
New York, NY 10036   (212) 391-0120

National Association of Area Agencies on Aging
600 Maryland Avenue, S.W.
West Wing, Suite 208
Washington, D.C. 20024   (202) 484-7520

National Association of State Units on Aging
2033 K Street, N.W.
Washington, D.C. 20006   (202) 785-0707

National Center for Home Equity Conversion
110 East Main Street, Room 605
Madison, WI 53703   (608) 256-2111

National Citizen's Coalition for Nursing Home Reform
1424 16th Street, N.W.
Washington, D.C. 20036   (202) 797-0657

National Council on Aging
600 Maryland Avenue, S.W., West Wing 100
Washington, D.C. 20024   (202) 479-1200

National Institute of Insurance Commissioners
1025 Connecticut Avenue, N.W.
Washington, D.C. 20036   (202) 223-7857

National Senior Citizen Law Center
2025 M Street, N.W., Suite 400
Washington, D.C. 20036   (202) 887-5280

Shared Housing Resource Center
6344 Greene Street
Philadelphia, PA 19144   (215) 848-1220

United Seniors' Health Cooperative
1334 G Street, N.W., Suite 500
Washington, D.C. 20005   (202) 393-6222

INDEX

166